THE HOMECOMING AND OTHER STORIES

THE HOMECOMING AND OTHER STORIES

PRADIP KUMAR DAS

PARTRIDGE
A Penguin Company

Partridge books may be ordered through booksellers or by contacting:

Partridge India
Penguin Books India Pvt.Ltd
11, Community Centre, Panchsheel Park, New Delhi 110017
India
www.partridgepublishing.com
Phone: 000.800.10062.62

CONTENTS

To

Aditya, Pramit,
Ashidhara and Shatabdi
On our 50th Wedding Anniversary

THE HOMECOMING AND OTHER STORIES

"If ever you are lucky enough to belong somewhere, if a place takes you in and you take it into yourself you don't desert it just because it can kill you. There are things more valuable in life." (Poppy Brite—The Lord of Nerves)

PREFACE

This book is a sequel to an earlier series of memoirs published in 2003, under the title "A Scent of Clover". Like the earlier stories, these observations, based on actual experience, are my own and intensely personal. They reflect my views on the demographic and other socio economic changes which have unwittingly taken their toll on the environment in which we currently live and work. Some of these changes are sad, some thought provoking, even threatening, and others, plain hilarious. Some sections are more philosophic and introspective, although, hopefully, not too didactic. The last chapter was written following a cherished visit to Angkor Wat in Cambodia with its profound riches. The book celebrates sixteen years in Calcutta, after our return to a city which has alternately mystified and horrified me and will, I hope, prove entertaining.

Pradip Kumar Das
Kolkata, 2013

CHAPTER 1

The Homecoming

My first impressions on returning to Calcutta (Kolkata) after an absence of almost 30 years was that the city was badly in need of repair, not just the physical aspects, but that in totality it presented an image of disinheritance and chaos not found in any other comparable Indian city, much less, elsewhere in the world. Frustration, fear insecurity and mindless violence had overtaken the so called intellectual and cultural superiority of the locals in virtually every walk of life. Insularity, arrogance and lethargy had become the bywords of a society fed on political propaganda and misplaced convictions. The absence of morality and ethics was conspicuous. It seemed unreal somehow to equate all this with the Bengali 'ethos' of civility and culture on which many of us had been bred.

In the spring of 1997 my Mother lay dying. She said she was happy her days were over because she could not bring herself to identify with the values or lifestyles of a generation which chose to deny its roots. A woman of exemplary equanimity and poise, she clung to her beliefs until the very end. Unable to cope with her own loneliness, she finally surrendered to the afflictions of her body. One evening, when Calcutta was going through one of its routine power cuts, she turned on her side and quietly breathed her last, symbolically, in the light of a flickering candle.

My wife and I were alone now, alone in the house in which my parents had lived for over four decades since my father's retirement from the ICS. It was a house full of incredible memories and I suppose I was fortunate enough to have inherited a legacy envied by many of my peers. My father had preceded my mother by four years and I had lost both sets of grandparents over the last few decades. My older brother, two years my senior, had chosen to settle in the US never to return. Neither he nor his American wife had developed any attachments to the family property in Jubilee Park.

In the fifties of the last century, Jubilee Park was surrounded by a large mango grove, all part of the erstwhile estate of the late Prince Gholam Mohammed Shah, 11th son of Tipu Sultan of the royal house of Mysore. Opposite our house in an unpretentious grave, lay the body of a mystic Sufi saint (Pugla Baba) who came to settle in the area more than 350 years ago. The grave, a symbolic conception of life, was lit, as late as the 1960s, by oil lamps after dusk and attracted devotees by some excellent *Qawal* singing on Thursday nights. Tollygunge was earlier known as Russapugla. Some say the name was derived from the Russa tree which grew in abundance in the locality and others from Rausa Pugla or the road to the shrine of Hazrat Maqsood Ghazi, alias Pugla (mad) Pir (saint) Baba who was reputed to possess remarkable powers. Nobody knows quite how the Pir Baba came to settle here more than 350 years ago. When Col. Tolly of the East India Company was allowed to dredge the waterway connecting the Hooghly to the Matla river system of East Bengal the area developed into a market or "gunge" for all shipping that passed through it. An elderly Eurasian couple with Portuguese origins who owned our house before emigrating to Australia, sold it to my father for a song. Neither they nor my father ever looked back. The surrounding greenery was a haven for wildlife, including the rare white owl and a variety of tropical birds. I had never seen a white owl before, but my mother and grandmother did—on the morning of the day we were married. It was supposed to be a very auspicious omen. According to reports, one flew down and sat on our compound wall for almost two hours, patiently enduring their conch blowing and ceremonial incantations to invoke Lakshmi, the Goddess of Wealth. Judging by later events, I suppose there is something to be said for prayer. The white owl ceased to be a rarity shortly afterwards. When we moved to Chennai we discovered two that lived in a large raintree in the compound of our house on Haddows road. They periodically made their appearance when they thought we needed the blessings of their Divine rider, which we frequently did. Her blessings certainly gave us much strength and stayed with us for many years afterwards.

To return to the days when we first moved to Tollygunge, you needed quite a bit of pluck living in, and driving to, the area. The main Russa Road (now Deshpran Sasmal Road) was no more than a narrow cobbled street with open drains on either side which overflowed during the monsoons. Tram tracks down the middle of the road were an added impediment. Prominent members of the Mysore royal family who had been exiled by the British to Calcutta after the Vellore Mutiny of 1807 had been allotted residential plots of land in the district. Notable among them was Prince Gholam Mohammed Shah whose palace, Pul Pahar, with its adjacent Imambara and Mosque were prominent landmarks. The Prince himself lived until 1878 during which time he ingratiated himself sufficiently with the Colonial government to earn among other things, a KCSI (Knight Commander of the Star of India) a nomination as Foundation Fellow to the University of Calcutta and a dinner meeting with Queen Victoria in London. More importantly he acquired property rights over 120 acres of land held by the East India Company including a large two storied house and several smaller houses later to be identified as the Tollygunge Club. Gholam Mohammed's brothers in exile were less fortunate. Most died intestate, while the more impoverished ones set up small businesses as traders and craftspersons throughout the length of the road as far as the railway bridge. Their presence and the influence of Islam in the locality was palpable. On festival days, especially Mohurrum and the biannual Urs, the encroachments were sufficient to bring all vehicular traffic to a standstill. If you were fortunate to own a car, you had to ensure it had a good horn and good brakes. Seatbelts were unheard of. So were traffic lights.

An early acquaintance was a scion of the Sultan's family who ran a decrepit looking motor garage out of his ancestral home on Anwar Shah Road. He was known in the neighbourhood as Munna or Munna bhai, a commonplace kind of name which concealed his actual identity. It was only at the wedding of his daughter, Nishat Ara, that we learnt of his parentage and family name, a name he shared with an illustrious predecessor, Sayed Ghulam Mohammed Shah. The title Sayed was much respected in his community. It signified a person of high rank and birth. Munna could not afford to maintain the sprawling Victorian Gothic mansion he had inherited, so he let out portions of it to a civil contractor, an auto electric repairer, an upholstery maker and a metal polisher. His own workmen were trained on the job to perform all manner of automobile repairs including dent removing, welding, painting and of course mechanical servicing of motor cars and two wheelers of all kinds. His workshop consisted of the backyard of his house and a few makeshift tin sheds. More often than not the work was shoddy, necessitating a second and even a third visit to Munna's garage, but he never once protested. Instead he would offer to repeat the job free of cost if necessary and, to assuage frayed tempers, steaming cups of tea, served by the local vendor in disposable clay cups (khuris) would follow. His frustrations forced Munna to drink, so when the house was sold to a promoter and his business needed to close down for good, he would invariably find his way to the local watering hole. On one such visit, he was so inebriated that he had difficulty crossing the road. Not unexpectedly, he was knocked down by a passing vehicle and had to be hospitalised. Fortunately he survived with his life.

Tipu Sultan and his descendants were Sunni Muslims. A few of them were buried in the mosque adjacent to Munna's house and some others in the cemetery just off Hazra Park Prince Gholam Mohammed Shah himself chose to be interned in the mosque premises. His grave, on a high raised plinth commensurate with the main building, is singularly austere with grass growing all around it and without even a marble slab to designate the spot where he was buried. The only indication of his burial is an Urdu inscription on one side of his grave, identifying the Prince's name and year of death. Time had obviously stood still for this section of the Mysore royals. From the debris of Mysore House when it was pulled down, I was able to salvage some rare ceramic floor tiles of the period which, even today, adorn our little garden in Jubilee Park. They will forever remind me of Munna Bhai's garage.

*   *   *

Another set of royals to be associated with the culture of the city was the ruler of Awadh, Wajid Ali Shah. Fifty years after the despatch of Tipu's descendants as hostages to Calcutta, the British annexed Oudh (Awadh) in 1856. Wajid Ali Shah and his family, were exiled and settled in one of the southern extremities of the city, Metia Burz (literally, "The Earthen Fort."). They were Shiite Muslims and the name Metia Burz derives from the raised earthen platform on which were built a series of fine houses with gardens rolling down

to the Hooghly. Wajid Ali Shah died in 1887 and his
beloved Metia Burz, like his palaces in Awadh, were
razed to the ground by the British after his death. Long
after the plunder and devastation, in 1982, a marble
plaque was put up on the gateway leading to Wajid Ali
Shah's Imambara where he lies interned, by the British
High Commissioner for India Sir John Thompson.
The plaque commemorates the "historic reconciliation"
that is supposed to have taken place "in a spirit of
mutual generosity." Be that as it may, Metia Burz grew
to be a centre of considerable cultural importance.
Troops of artistes, among them Jadu Bhatta of the
Vishnupur Gharana and Aghorenath Chakravarti, both
classical Dhrupad singers, Sajjad Mohammad (sitar)
Dhirendranath Bose (sarod) Shyam Lal Goswami and
Rai Chand Boral were prominent. The Nawab, himself a
talented performer, learnt Hindustani vocal music from
Basit Khan, Pyar Khan and Jaffar Khan and trained as
a Kathak dancer under Thakur Prasadji and Binadin
Maharaj. He also composed lyrics, thumries and ghazals
under the pen name Akhtar Piya, some of which, like
"Jab Chhor Chali Lucknow Nagari, "Neer Bhararana
Main Kaise Jaun" and "Babul Mora, Naihar Chhuto hi
Jai" have become immortal in the annals of Hindustani
classical music. This was also the time when one of the
most famous women classical vocalists the country has
produced—Gauhar Jan—made Calcutta her home. The
burgeoning wealth of the city during the period gave rise
to a group of upper class gentlemen (revenue collectors
or *Zamindars*) who owed allegiance to the British, and
some others, engaged in the lucrative opium trade, who
patronised this culture and gave Calcutta its aura of
gentility and aesthetic sensibility.

I was curious to find out a little more about the family and finally managed to meet one of Wajid Ali Shah's great grandsons, Nayyer Quder at the Sibtenabad Imambara of Metia Burz. The Imambara was built in 1864 and is approached by an imposing gateway with stuccoed fish emblems, similar in many ways to one of the gateways of the Kaiserbagh Palace in Lucknow. According to another surviving descendant, Asifjah Mohammed, the fish was adopted by the rulers of Awadh as an emblem of good fortune after Awadh was won by Wajid Ali Khan's predecessor, Nawab Sadat Khan. Apparently a fish jumped up from the river onto the Nawab's lap as he was sailing towards his new kingdom. A priest accompanying the party saw this as a good omen and felt that if the Nawab let it go back to the water, his wish would be granted. The Imambara itself is a modest whitewashed building with scalloped arches and a flat ceiling from which hang rare crystal chandeliers and lamps. Wajid Ali Shah and many of his family members are buried there, dominated by the Awadhi Coat of Arms, a flaming sun, carrying a shield with crossed swords, the whole flanked by two mermaids. Nayyer Quder currently lives in London's Grosvenor Square, but visits the shrine his ancestors built, once a year.

*   *   *

Apologists for Calcutta and other loyalist groups claim that Calcutta was "different" in the "old days." How different, is a matter of opinion. My earliest memories, as a child visiting the city, were of a set of doting maternal grandparents who were constantly

falling over backwards to ensure my older brother and
I had a good time spending our annual school holidays
with them. This included all kinds of treats including
specialities cooked by my grandmother, walks to the
Lakes (now known as Rabindra Sarobar) in company
with my grandfather, occasional visits to the Zoo, and
lunch at Calcutta's Peiping Restaurant followed by a
Matinee film show. They lived in a small two storied
house on Kankulia Road (now Ballygunge Gardens), a
labyrinthian colony of residential buildings interlaced
by narrow streets. They were both enlightened folk. My
grandfather, Dr. Nagendramohan Gupta renounced
his orthodox Hindu background in Sonargaon, East
Bengal (now Bangladesh) to graduate from the Benaras
Hindu University. From there he was able to secure a
grant from the Raja of Tajhat to study in Japan and
afterwards, through the munificence of an Austrian
woman admirer, he travelled by sea to Vienna to write a
thesis in organic Chemistry. He received his Ph.d. degree
from the University of Vienna at the hands of Kaiser
Wilhelm II himself. Nagendramohan was fluent in both
Japanese and German. As children we were fascinated
by the stories of his many adventures. On return to
India, Nagendramohan was asked by the elders of his
community to perform *prayashchitta* a form of oblation
to wash off the sins associated with crossing the Kala
Pani or Black Waters. This involved among other things,
the ingestion of bovine urine. When Nagendramohan
refused he was excommunicated from his faith and
embraced the beliefs of the Brahmo Samaj, a Hindu
reformist movement started by Raja Rammohan Roy,
without actually becoming a practising member. His
professional career ended as Principal of the Normal

Training College in Rangpur, an institution to train teachers in specific areas of specialisation like Science education, Mathematics, Art and Physical Education. It was part of an all India programme launched by the British Government but the position did not do justice to the man or his qualifications. My grandmother, Jyotirmoyee, had a remarkable and prodigious memory. As one of the first women graduates of Calcutta's Bethune College she could—as just one notable example—recite the whole of Michael Madhusudan Dutt's "Meghnad Badh Kabya" without pausing. There were numerous others. She wrote a number of delightful childrens' stories, doubtless to entertain us, but it was a talent she could have exploited professionally. Her cooking left us ecstatic. She always used the best ingredients, turning up her nose at anything which was not fried in pure *ghee*. During her active years she too was involved with education, as an Inspectress of Schools, in Rangpur. Jyotirmoyee's father, Sasadhar Ray was an erudite and well read person of his day. One of his quotes (from Emerson) which, lasted me a lifetime was about the quality of greatness. "True greatness", he used to say, "does not lie in never falling, but in rising each time you fall."

My grandparents lived modestly but well, within the limits of my grandfather's pension. For want of help, Nagendramohan spent his spare time polishing the brass in his house, including the brass nameplate which bore his name, on the front door. He rarely wore Western clothes but when he did he looked elegant in his suits, some of which sported labels with the names of London's well known West End tailors. At home, he always wore a dhoti and kurta. I never saw Jyotirmoyee in anything other than a sari. Unlike her husband, she was a devout Hindu and spent a major portion of her day in prayer. One corner of their balcony on the first floor was converted to my grandmother's puja room where she lit the ceremonial lamp each evening and made her daily offerings of flowers and *bhog* (edibles) to Vishnu, the family deity.

The house on Kankulia Road overlooked many of the apartments occupied by my grandparents' neighbours. We hardly ever met them, although once in a while, conversations took place from adjoining balconies or across the street. Although born as one, the Bengali psyche has never ceased to intrigue me. It was disgusting enough that the neighbours routinely threw their garbage out on the street, in total disregard of the environment or passers by. Nor could I relate to the kind of exhibitionism which required an individual to perambulate from room to room while brushing their teeth or better still, in the open. It seemed as much a part of the middle class Bengali ethos then, as it is now. Most middle class families also opted for the *Choubaccha* an open air water reservoir used by members of the household to take a bath. In the absence of electric water pumps in many houses, they served among other things to conserve water and to segregate the toilet, considered "impure", from the bathing area. Users would stand in front of the *choubaccha* in full view of their neighbours with nothing more than a *gamcha* or thin towel and/or a sari wrapped round their bare bodies Most of them were corpulent men and women, although once in a while there were flashes of sinewy young flesh. Either way, the sight was not particularly edifying. Instead it contributed majorly to the sense of alienation between viewer and subject.

Pavements were used then, as they are now, by whole families as living spaces, to sleep, cook, wash and bathe. Calcutta's decibel levels were always high, cows wandered all over its streets and traffic was chaotic. It was the home of all kinds of epidemics from cholera to malaria and small pox. Its beggar and fly menace were prophetic. Even the semi naked thela (handcart) and rickshaw pullers have continued for decades in the shadow of Bengali sentimentalism. I never heard of another city in India whose streets were washed down daily, although loyal Calcuttans who, like me, remember the hydrants and hose pipes of that period, say this with characteristic nostalgia. In retrospect, Calcutta's thoroughfares were obviously so filthy as to warrant daily flushing! Needless to add they didn't remain clean for long. The washing stopped soon after Independence and today the Calcuttan takes his city's filth and garbage for granted.

Not long ago, the well known German novelist Gunter Grass and his wife Ute were in Calcutta. On a visit to the National Library they were apalled not only by the manner in which books and rare manuscripts were kept and treated but by the "primal stench" of the men's toilet right next to the cafeteria and the pile of sanitary napkins strewn on the floor of the women's toilet. They wondered what compelled the "studious young ladies of Bengal, always fresh as blossoms in their saris" to act in this unbelievably revolting manner. With hygiene and health care going down the tube at every street corner, one wonders what it is that brings a sparkle to every Bengali eye at the very mention of his native city.

I tried, but failed to analyse the mystique of Calcutta. Why were people attracted to it? One clue was the intellectual and cultural revival of the 19th and early 20th centuries with such household names as Raja Ram Mohan Roy, Dwarakanath Thakur, Ishwar Chandra Vidyasagar, Bankim Chandra Chatterjee Michael Madhusudan Dutt and Swami Vivekananda. Their sayings and writings represented all that is close to the Bengali heart while at the same time freeing the mind of narrow prejudice and irrationality, at least among a section of the Bengali intelligentsia. It was a phenomenon unique to Calcutta coinciding as it did with the Nationalist movement. The other is that in the last few decades before and after Independence, the city produced as many as four Nobel Laureates and at least one scientist, Jagadish Chandra Bose, who narrowly missed the honour because the Royal Society of Britain refused to recognise an important aspect of his work.

But more than all of this, it was undoubtedly the multifaceted genius of Bengal's very own Rabindranath Tagore that has, over the last 150 years, impacted the culture of Bengal like no other, Tagore's poetry, his lyrics, his prose short stories and plays focussed on every imaginable aspect of the Bengali psyche and the fact that his active creative life coincided with the Freedom movement gave the Bengali ethos a whole new dimension. What is perhaps lesser known is that Rabindranath Tagore too, denounced the weaknesses of our national character in words of one syllable. This lesser known address was delivered in 1895 on the occasion of a Memorial service for Pandit Ishwarchandra Vidyasagar and I quote: "We begin but never finish, we make a show but we do nothing concrete, we do not believe what we set out to do, what we believe we do not carry out, we spin out words without end but cannot make the smallest sacrifice, we feel pleased with ourselves for exhibiting our pride but never think it is necessary to be worthy, we depend on others for everything and rend the skies finding fault with them. We take pride in imitating others, we feel honoured to receive their favours yet we throw dust in their eyes and call it politics; and the main object of our lives is to make clever speeches that fill us with self admiration."

*   *   *

The British presence coupled with the Second World War and the impending threat of a Japanese invasion helped to maintain a degree of law and order which, today, is much prized. However, this was eclipsed by the Bengal famine of 1943/44 during which an estimated 4 million people lost their lives. After the War and, nearer Independence, the Hindu-Muslim riots of 1946, also known as the Great Calcutta Killings,—a savage and brutal blood bath which lasted for four days and nights and accounted for approximately 7000 dead and several more wounded. In the former case, emaciated destitutes in their thousands flooded Calcutta from the neighbouring rural areas of Bengal, looking for food. They were peasants and village families who were forced to sell off their land because of a crop failure and stringent follow up action by the British Government to siphon off available supplies to feed their troops on the Burmah front. The resultant devastation saw human indignity at its lowest, with men women and children picking food from dustbins and castaway hospital waste. They died like flies on the city's pavements crying out for a little succour. The second was an orgy of mob violence, looting and massacre involving both Hindus and Muslims. From the terrace of our house on Loudon Street we could see columns of black smoke rising from Mullick Bazar as it went up in flames while cries of Allah-o-Akbar and Jai Shri Bajrangbali rent the air. The street battles and gang warfares that followed were spectacles of remorseless violence with pitchforks, lathis, knives and choppers thrown in. I vividly recall our Hindu milkman staggering up to the gate of the house with an ugly looking butcher's knife stuck to his back. He collapsed and bled to death right there in front of our eyes. I was all of eight then.

The Japanese bombed Calcutta in 1944/45 and there were reports of Japanese troops advancing on land towards Rangoon and Mandalay. Shiploads carrying hundreds of Indian families settled in Burma, set sail for Calcutta. Others less fortunate walked all the way to safety across the Arakan mountains into Imphal and Manipur in India. I clearly remember the sand bags stacked in the glass fronted lobby of our house on Harish Mukherjee Road to prevent possible shards of flying glass with each explosion, the wailing sirens, and the dull boom-boom of ack ack fire as the enemy planes approached. Public monuments like the Victoria Memorial were painted black to avoid detection at night and motor car headlights across the city were masked. Dennis Rao then a young man in his late teens came to work for us as a domestic help in 1946. A native of Andhra, his family had settled in Mandalay. When hostilities broke out he took to the road with his relatives and walked for a month to reach the nearest American base where he was hired as personal orderly to Major James Bardwell of the US Infantry. Later when the unit moved back to Calcutta to be disbanded, Dennis accompanied them to find alternative employment.

Without going into the reasons, these and earlier events gave Calcutta the somewhat dubious and unenviable reputation of being known as the city of refugees and agitations. The description was not entirely baseless. The turn of events following the Indigo Revolt of 1861 or the effects of Curzon's shortlived Partition of Bengal are too well known to require elaboration. 1926 saw another major skirmish between Hindus and Muslims after a Hindu procession was attacked by Muslims as it was passing a mosque during its call to prayer, ignoring the latter's appeal not to play loud music in deference to Islamic religious sanctions. Communal tensions continued for several years afterwards. In 1930 the British Inspector of Prisons was shot dead at point blank range in his office in Calcutta's Writers Buildings by three Bengali revolutionaries, Benoy, Badal and Dinesh while the decade preceding the outbreak of the Second World War was taken up by the repercussions of Gandhi's agitation for Independence coupled with the anti Imperialist movement and actions initiated by Subhas Chandra Bose. The events of the last thirty years, some bordering on anarchy, coupled with a total breakdown of law and order have only strengthened this impression.

*   *   *

In the fifties there was still a sizeable population of Europeans in the city and I suppose I was in a way fortunate to have been a part of the country's Indianisation process. Racial tensions had eased and as a teenager on the brink of adulthood it was exciting to be able to mix on equal terms with a breed of people most Indians held in some awe. This was possible through an English friend who had come out to Calcutta to take charge of the American Express office on Old Court House Street. He was a young, good looking bachelor who in due course adopted my mother as his own and was therefore welcome in our house. Douglas Castle was a few years older than I. He had numerous girl friends, among them Moira Jervis, daughter of Burmah Shell's Eastern Regional Manager, P.A. Jervis. They lived in a large colonial mansion in Alipore served by a retinue of servants and hosted lavish parties to which I was invited as part of the family. Moira's mother, a regal and elegant woman in her mid fifties was nicknamed "The Duchess." She certainly looked and acted like one. Many years later as a student in England I was invited to visit their home in Bray, Maidenhead, a large, quintessentially English, cottage surrounded by woods. I spent many weekends with Douglas in his own two roomed apartment on Chowringhee where I met many of his other English and European friends and was initiated among other things into smoking expensive foreign cigarettes and sipping my first ever Gin and tonic. On Saturdays we would invariably end up dining and watching a cabaret show at Prince's, Grand Hotel or the Palm Court at Scherezade, another elegant party venue under the stars with dancing and a live band playing soft music. Black ties and dinner jackets were of course *de rigueur* at both places. Some of the shows were spectacular. I especially recall three—a group of Can-Can dancers straight out of the Moulin Rouge in Paris, Belly dancers Lyn and Lys from Cairo and a brilliant male tenor from the US whose take off of the more popular Frank Sinatra numbers was the closest thing I've heard to listening to the great man live. On other nights we just ended up at Nizam's for a *kathi* roll. Douglas came from a modest home in London's Clapham Common. He had no chips on his shoulders and no pretensions.

Another colourful personality who regularly visited our home was a Scotsman, Jimmy Moncur, from Dundee. Jimmy lived and worked out of the Agarpara Jute Mills where he proudly proclaimed his designation in flawless Hindi, as "Krani saab" (krani as in kerani, a lowly paid clerk). Jimmy took his Scottish country dancing classes very seriously indeed and often appeared wearing his traditional kilt and sporran. These classes were held in St Andrews Church, Dalhousie Square, where most Calcutta based Scotsmen congregated. Scottish country dancing was also regularly practised at the Scottish Club on Gokhale Road opposite the house where my in-laws lived. On another occasion Jimmy waded through knee deep rain water to come home for a meal. Like Douglas, Jimmy was also a bachelor and something of an Indophile with spiritual interests. He continued to be a loyal friend and wrote to my parents for many years after leaving Calcutta for good. His uncomplicated and simple soul demanded that he be present at our wedding with an expensive Chinese hand painted vase and plate as a gift.

A third visitor to our home was Michael Brisby. He started out as an official of the British Ministry of Steel when my father was posted as Secretary, Commerce and Industries to the Government of West Bengal but in time became a close friend of my parents. His beautiful wife Liliana was Bulgarian, with green eyes and a shock of blonde hair. Amita and I visited their home in South Kensington after we were married. Before that he took us to lunch at "Greens" a fashionable English restaurant just off Piccadilly. One of the reasons why we remember Michael very fondly was that on one of his visits to neighbouring Bangladesh he took the trouble to post 4 tins of "Ostermilk" for Aditya, then only a few months old, because baby food was in short supply in Calcutta.

My own friends around this time were Arup Mukherji and Partha Basu, not counting old school friends from Delhi like Sandip Dutta and Debabrata (Bachhoo) Sengupta, who periodically descended on Calcutta to visit family. My father was on transfer and the fact that I was uprooted in my final year at school from St. Columba's in Delhi where I was preparing to sit the Senior Cambridge examination in December, 1953, had proved to be a major trauma. Besides adjusting to an entirely new set of teachers and academic disciplines the Cambridge syllabus followed by my new school, La Martiniere, was very different. I had to take on new subjects like Mechanics (a variation of Statics and Dynamics) and to digest a different set of text books prescribed for English Literature. The culture at my new school was also very different. The building, very different from red brick St Columba's, was an elegant Palladian type structure from Colonial India with a rotunda of Tuscan pillars and a flight of steps leading to the main portico which once supported a dome and housed a chapel. The school was named after a Frenchman, Major General Claude Martin, a Military engineer, at the court of Wajid Ali Shah, erstwhile ruler of Awadh. The mother institution, in Lucknow, was an older and grander18[th] century establishment named "Constantia", which served as Claude Martin's residence until he died. It played a role in the Defence of Lucknow during the Uprising of 1857 and was bequeathed by Martin to the State to be converted into a boys' school, as were his other properties in Lyon, France, and of course in Calcutta. Curiously though, French at which I had become pretty proficient by this time, was not an option at La Martiniere. I had to find a tutor for private lessons. One of the clauses in Martin's Will was that the school would fund the education and maintenance of groups of Foundationers—poor, but promising, Eurasian students who could not afford the luxury of a liberal education. Some of these students took advantage of the scheme to turn the institution into a home for under privileged boys of Eurasian descent. They routinely failed their school leaving examinations and grew into young adult males at the school's expense. They were a law unto themselves and usually ended up as Prefects by virtue of their seniority and excellence at sports, especially Rugby, a game initiated in England

and named after the famous Public School of that
name. Annual Rugby matches between the Martinieres
of Lucknow and Calcutta were standard. Overall the
experience of transferring from a Jesuit education to a
Protestant school with a different set of ethics, values
and priorities was unsettling.

Neither Arup, nor Partha nor I were rugby playing types.
We left school together to join St Xavier's College. After
completing the University Intermediate Examination,
Arup and I left St Xavier's to join Calcutta's Presidency
College to read History. Partha opted to study
Commerce and ultimately to qualify as a Chartered
Accountant. Arup's father was Docks Manager at
Calcutta Port. He was a fun loving gentleman always
ready to take us on outings and treats. One of the places
he loved to visit was Nizam's, the kabab shop, where
I tasted my first "khiri" roll. On one vacation he also
arranged for all of us to travel to Vishakhapatnam,
where I had my first ever glimpse of the ocean. Arup's
family were Indian Christians. He had two younger
sisters and the family lived in the upstairs flat of a
spacious Government bungalow in Portland Park. I
remember the house well not only because I visited it
often but because in 1962, the year I returned to India
after completing my studies in England, I stayed with
his parents for almost two weeks while the Jubilee Park
house was being renovated. Arup was a very talented
pianist. Besides qualifying for the LTCL and the FTCL
from the Trinity College of Music, London he took part
in several music competitions where he would invariably
emerge as the winner. Arup and I left for England after
graduation. Arup went to Christ Church Oxford and I

found myself at the London School of Economics trying unsuccessfully to juggle a second Bachelor's degree with periodic shots at the Indian Administrative Service examination in the hope of following in my father's footsteps. Both Arup and I finally graduated once more in England and went into industry. Arup joined a large Consumer products' company and I found a promising opening with a British oil company. We both learned to drive together.

Partha came from a distinguished family of North Calcutta. There was a time when almost every afternoon, Partha would ride home on the bar of my bicycle from St Xavier's College to our house, then on Lee Road. It was a spacious colonial type two storied building with a garden, typical of pre Independence Calcutta, south of Park Street, which the Government "requisitioned" when my father was transferred from New Delhi in 1951. We lived on the first floor. The ground floor was occupied by an Englishman, one of the last of the expatriates to serve the Calcutta Electric Supply Company. In the bedlam of commercialisation, which in the last decade or so has completely transformed these quiet residential areas into glitzy shopping arcades and offices, the house still stands, with an added floor, but perhaps the only remaining one of its kind on that property. Partha was more the introspective sort always interested in the creative arts and fancied writing in his spare time. Starting out as a poet he soon matured into a creative writer and is today an author and literary critic. Another friendship which matured after we were married, was with a young couple, about our age or slightly younger—Martin and Carolyn Karcher. He was

French and she was Jewish American. In 1965, Martin was posted to Calcutta with the World Bank and had instructions to meet and interview me for a position in the Bank's Young Executives programme. I failed to qualify but found two great friends. Like the others, this attachment continues.

My other interest at this time was classical music—an addiction which was to last a lifetime. Other than my Mother who regularly sang and practised the sitar at home, I was totally mesmerised by a Ravi Shankar concert which I attended with my parents, at New Delhi's Constitution Club. Ravi Shankar, then in his twenties, was already a leading artist on All India Radio and a rising star. The venue was no more than a collection of hutments situated on Old Mill Road (now Rafi Marg) near Connaught Place. There could not have been more than about 50 people at the concert. Everyone sat on the floor *baithak* style and the more seasoned afficionados were at best patronising in their praise for the young artist. Calcutta, on the other hand presented a vast and varied canvass of performers, players and singers from all over India. Its all night Music Conferences held across the city attempted to lure the best musicians in their respective disciplines. They included such legendary names as Pandit Omkarnath Thakur, Hirabai Barodekar, Ustad Bade Ghulam Ali Khan, Ustad Amir Khan, the Dagar Brothers, Ustad Allauddin Khan, Ustad Keramatullah Khan, Pandit Shanta Prasad, Pandit Chatur Lal, Ustad Alla Rakha, Ustad Mohd. Sagiruddin, Birju Maharaj, Sitara Devi, Begum Akhtar and among the younger artists, Ravi Shankar, Ali Akbar Khan and Vilayat

Khan. There were many others. My interest in classical music started out as curiosity and has still not ended. Calcutta's Music Conferences attracted the musical cognocenti and glitterati of the city, including some of the city's most beautiful women. One of them, Rani Ray, daughter of Raja Birendrakishore Roychoudhuri of Gouripur—himself a master of the Dhrupad style who played the Been, the Sursingar and the Seni Rabab—was a well known beauty of her time. She made waves in the society of her day and was a regular at all of Ravi Shankar's concerts. I was privileged to visit their house on Ballygunge Circular Road a few times to participate in typical salon type *addas* where everyone sat crosslegged on a carpeted floor with bolsters for support to discuss and debate all manner of subjects from the esoteric to the intensely practical. My companion at these gatherings was a childhood friend turned painter, Ayesha alias 'Tutu' Lahiri who had converted her tiny apartment on Fern Road into a veritable atelier. She worked late into the night with colours and subjects in a style vaguely reminiscent of Amrita Sher-Gill.

*   *   *

Then as now, the emphasis on plain living and high thinking were the twin props of Bengali chauvinism. It was a culture sustained by an inherited assumption of its own superiority. The Bengali ethos, was built on the belief that Bengalis are somehow the ground base of society with no time for abstractions like the needs of the state or good citizenship. It was a curious mixture of the romanticism of Rabindranath, the stark realities of Jibananda Das and the contributions by

Bengali revolutionaries to the Freedom Movement Unaccustomed as I was to these pretensions, the experience was at times novel, at times interesting and at times slightly uncomfortable. It meant accepting a set of values and a landscape which to some of us was unfamiliar but which the majority of Bengalis seemed to inhabit without much strain.

Today, Bengal is more defensive than arrogant. The conspicuous mediocrity of its people is palpable. The majority of its so-called celebrities in the arts and culture segment—our poets, writers theatre workers and film makers—are either septuagenerians or octogenarians. Thanks to the inflow of migrants from rural areas, and our neighbouring states, coupled with relatively easy social mobility, a new breed consisting of lumpen elements both in the middle and working classes have secured a stranglehold on trade unions, jobs in the bureaucracy and academia. They are politically assertive, with little respect for ethics or the rule of law. Their education, vision, ability to rethink and tackle problems is very different. They make a show of espousing the cause of the poor and the downtrodden while at the same time lining their own pockets. They think nothing of clothes hung out to dry on street dividers, or people relieving themselves with abandon in public places. They turn a blind eye to the routine accumulation of garbage at street corners and come out with the most extraordinary defence of inconseqential issues. This is the new face of the State's leadership. If at University we argued about the erosion of ideologies among the Bengali intelligentsia, it is happening now in front of our eyes.

Within these complex demographic changes, the contradictions of the Bengali psyche have continued—supreme unconcern over individual harassment and suffering, and mob violence following a road accident or a failed football match. Nor is it clear why successful Bengali professionals unlike their counterparts in other states deliberately choose to operate out of the most squalid surroundings in their private practice or why a Bengali home, even in a moderately well-to-do environment resembles a cluttered barn, warehouse and kitchen all rolled into one. The ubiquitous "adda" typifying Bengali lifestyles is, on its flip side, a senseless waste of time and a dubious addition to the quality of our lives. As for the younger generation what better testimony to their appreciation and taste than the opinion of a group of students sitting in the heartland of Bengali chauvinism, Shantiniketan's Viswa Bharati University. When asked who their ideals were, they unhesitatingly opted for Aishwariya Rai and Sachin Tendulkar without so much as a thought to the founder of the institution!

It is not easy for anyone to distance himself from his roots and I don't suppose I am an exception. At the same time as I grew into adulthood I found it increasingly difficult to relate to some of these values. My older brother, two years my senior and my mentor for over 15 years, was more forthright. He decided he wanted freedom above everything else and left for the US, never to return. In his own inimitable fashion he described it as a journey into darkness. There were problems of acceptance and non acceptance, belief and trust, faith, hope, want and desire in every society. He is still struggling for an identity.

Both my parents were relatively unconventional Hindus. My father, an only son, who lost his mother at the tender age of five, rebelled against his father, his caste and community in provincial Dhaka to marry my mother and set up a nuclear family. He was a brilliant student who left home to graduate from the Presidency College with a First Class Honours degree in Economics and the added distinction of being admitted to a Ph.d. programme at the London School of Economics on the basis of his Bachelor's degree alone. He then went on to sit for the combined Civil Services Examination in London competing against his English peers to join the small band of ICS officers who ruled India at that time. My mother was sixteen years old when she was married. The younger of two sisters, she was a woman of more than usual ability and perception. To steer clear of many of the stereotypical associations surrounding Westernised Indian society wives of her time, was not easy. In due course she developed a personality and set of values of her own, which some of her peers admired even as some others envied. My mother insisted on completing a University degree and set out to find herself through her painting and her music. Both my parents were voracious readers who found time to enjoy their individual spaces without letting themselves being sucked into the vortex of Club life and parties. They were an enlightened couple who believed in and practised non discrimination between religious beliefs and sexes. Behind the façade of the Civil Service my father was a very humane person and showed his support for the National movement in private. My mother accompanied Mahatma Gandhi to the areas affected by the 1946 communal riots and very often wore homespun cotton saris.

For the same reasons, and also because my father was on transferable service, we never got involved in the ups and downs of joint family living. My father's income was sufficient to pay for the best schools, and the large houses in which we lived were Government owned and maintained. At one time, our domestic staff consisted of a *bawarchi* (cook), a *masalchi* (cook's mate), two *khitmudgars* bearers, a chauffeur and a *jamadar* (sweeper), besides my father's personal orderly. As relics of the Raj, these colonial mansions had large manicured lawns, some with fruit trees, gravelled driveways, tennis courts and rose gardens. They were separately tended by groups of CPWD workmen. Not surprisingly we never felt the need for or missed family support. Indeed relatives would frequently approach my father for assistance with college admissions or suitable jobs. Our medical expenses were paid for by Government. So was travel, when my father was on official duty. Despite the charms of many of Calcutta's joint families, we led undisturbed lives free of family intrigue and squabbles. Indeed, my brother and I had a cosmopolitan upbringing. Our friends were drawn from all over India and we learnt to live with and appreciate customs, practices and beliefs very different from our own. On its flip side, we were slotted into the category of "sahibs" by the Bengali intelligentsia. I guess it was an attitude problem born basically out of insularity and ignorance, and more importantly, the Bengali penchant for envy.

What did puzzle me then, although I understand better now, is that the very people who levelled such criticisms at us also secretly dreamt of a Western lifestyle. All of us were products of a colonial education system which aimed not at a child's holistic development but to select the best in competition with each other with the ultimate object of serving the Empire. The ICS was of course at the apex of this pyramid. It was known as "the heaven born service" and "the steel frame of the British Empire". To belong to the ICS, regardless of individual loyalties was to belong to an exclusive club representing the crème de la crème of the brains of this country. In keeping with this culture of superiority the rulers made sure of the acceptance by the native population of the wide discrepancies between them and their British masters, not only at the domestic level but also at the commercial and mercantile levels where many Bengalis who paraded themselves as Bengal's landed gentry were in fact no more than agents of the colonisers. They made their fortunes as *Banias* to share the plunder of Bengal, lived in palatial mansions and ruthlessly exploited their own less privileged countrymen who were forced into bonded labour and eventually became their feudal subjects While some, like Dwarkanath Tagore combined the profit motive with acts of philanthropy and social purpose, and others like Bhudev Mukhopadhyay could retort that he was better off not shaking hands with a European because he would then need to take a bath, the more ignoble ones like Raja Nabakrishna Deb of Shovabazar, demonstrated his loyalty to the new icons of power, by having himself painted by Charles Coleman (a British artist) showing the Raja standing beside Clive on the plains of Plassey or by donating land for the building of Colonial Calcutta's first Anglican cathedral. Another painting depicts the Raja on the banks of the Hooghly bidding the Englishman goodbye.

His grandson, Radhakanta Deb hosted a lavish ball in the family Natmandir to celebrate the British victory in the Uprising of 1857. This was no ordinary party. Bearing in mind similar functions at Calcutta's Government House, he arranged to decorate the pavilion with "sumptuous carpets embroidered with gold" a golden throne and the royal standard of England. An estimated 300 guests attended the function. If such displays demonstrated wealth and status in the style of the Mughal court they were also the work of loyal British subjects, mimicking British material culture Let us discount, for the moment the lease by the Sabarna Roychoudhury family of the three villages of Sutanuti, Gobindopur and Kalikata at throwaway prices which led to the foundation of Colonial Calcutta, not to speak of the obsequiousness, treachery and intrigue that characterised Bengal under the Nawabs of Murshidabad.

*   *   *

The impact of British colonial culture was obviously profound. However, the litigious and extravagant nature of the heirs of the first generation of Bengali businessmen and their disenchantment arising out of several frauds perpetrated by East India Company representatives and others made joint ventures unattractive, not to speak of the existence of easy and lucrative avenues for investment in permanently settled zamindaris. The lack of an upcountry network contributed to this situation. But what perhaps was left unsaid was the misplaced Bengali belief about his own superior intelligence and unwillingness either to learn new skills or to perform tasks involving physical labour. These attitudes, at once egocentric and negative, have not helped to regenerate a state badly in need of initiatives. Nowhere is this more apparent than in the fatuous pronouncements of what one writer describes as Bengal's "babu-ocracy" who hold sway in the corridors of power. In fact it permeates the entire Bengali psyche, with echoes in family and everyday encounters, not to speak of professional life. Until a few years ago, Bengalis shunned manual labour. Virtually all Calcutta's taxi drivers were Sikhs and its handcart pushers, rickshaw pullers and porters, Biharis. Bengalis continue to excel as clerks in banks and government offices and as petty shopkeepers where there is scope for an afternoon siesta, unending cups of tea and occasional leisure strolls round the corner. I have lived in all four metros of this country and the difference is palpable. The desire basically to serve in return for a steady salary and a degree of security are weaknesses on which no colonial power could fail to capitalize. The British did just that. With no real engagement with the locals who were more than eager to please their foreign masters, they were happy to be waited upon.

It is curious that despite racial discrimination in all its forms, a section of Bengalis even today, claim custodianship of the ancient "heritage" and "traditions" left by the British more than 65 years ago. I have often asked myself what these terms mean. Do they convey the perpetuation of the myths and rumours floated by a group of British businessmen whose only reason to come to India was to make money? Or are these words a camouflage by their Indian successors to mask their own home grown exclusivity? The quintessential Imperial style of functioning was to set up institutions where the rulers could unwind without being overheard by the natives and sometimes even by their own wives. The British excluded Indians from membership of their clubs and confined the ladies to pursuits and locations appropriate to their interests and lifestyles. The men rode, took their horses to the bar, walked their dogs and went pig sticking. The ladies played croquet, tennis, swam and went to Fancy Dress parties. Their interests were certainly not in books, reading or local government. Do the present generation of Indians believe these values are worth preserving or, capable of imitation? For a start there are no "natives" to exclude! Secondly, membership profiles and mindsets have undergone a sea change. Information technology with all its ramifications has rubbished the colonial ethic of superiority and patronising tolerance. What then remains of "heritage" is a nebulous, undigested concoction of colonial "conventions" some of which have long outlived their usefulness or relevance.

Among members of the Bengali upper classes there are people who still wallow in expressions like the "aristocracy" of the colonial rulers, the "coveted cuisine" they introduced and the "fine architecture" of their buildings. These expressions, other than reflecting low self esteem, surely served to placate the new rulers at a time when the Mughal administration was in decay. They completely ignore the circumstances underlying the British conquest of this country—playing upon native weaknesses, especially their lack of cohesion and integrity—not just by military might but by a variety of guiles and subterfuges, to overawe the local population. The hybridity of this culture is mind boggling. Among other things, it manifested itself in manners, dress, cuisine and architecture. This conduct was legitimised by playing upon the altruistic elements of the Christian faith and, by contrast the "paganism" of the non believer. The ethic was very different from the language of the North American colonists for example, where the stakes were political and pitted against the British parliament. Following the collapse of the Mughal empire, it became necessary to keep Islam in check and to ensure that it did not pose a threat to Christian supremacy. The Hindu element was bought off by patronage and Western education. The "coveted cuisine" which is also frequently a topic of cocktail party conversations, was also largely concocted and a pale reflection of the original, complete with indigenous ingredients and spices. I refer, among many others, to the ubiquitous Bengali "chop" (very different from its English counterpart) or the *kabiraji* (coverage) cutlet and to many other items like the *pantheras* (a kind of stuffed crepe) or the cook's version of the Hamburger steak. Even the typical "puddings" we grew up with, like baked/boiled custards or the humble bread and butter pudding, which became standard fare in many Bengali households, have virtually disappeared from English menus. I have come across Fish 'Muniya' (Meuniere) at a Bengali wedding and 'tata' (tartare) sauce at one of Calcutta's leading Clubs.

*   *   *

Bengalis alternately despise and envy the other major community in the state—the Marwaris. The Marwaris came to Calcutta in sizeable numbers in the 1820s and soon became the city's most important trading community. By contrast to the Bengali *bhadralok* they believed in hard work. Shivnarain Birla the first in the clan to leave the family home in Pilani travelled on camel back across the Thar Desert for 20 days to reach Ahmedabad en route to Bombay. He lived in a cramped room with several others for over 20 years before moving into an apartment with more legroom. During this period he built up his fortune in speculative deals involving the opium trade. Nathuram Saraf, one of the first Marwari baniyas of Calcutta came to the city on a local river boat from Mirzapur as a part of its cargo. The journey usually took a few weeks and the deal was that the "passenger" would be responsible for the safe conduct of the rest of the cargo in return for food and a small remuneration. There are many similar examples. The Marwaris had a great support system. When a Marwari travelled on business his wife and children were cared for in a joint family at home. Outside home, he found shelter and good Marwari food in a *basa* a kind of cooperative inn supported by local Marwari merchants. Their sons and nephews were apprenticed to other Marwari traders and by and large they made maximum use of family networks, traditional accounting and financial controls. They started out as agents of British companies and ended up as independent business people. Discounting for the moment the well known and oft repeated refrain about their unethical business

practices, the Marwaris have always been a highly
disciplined and closely knit community. With complex
interlocking financial arrangements which helped them
to generate credit at every indigenous level they became
an indispensable part of trade and commerce in Colonial
Calcutta. Soon they established their presence in the
cloth, grain, oilseeds, raw jute, unprocessed goods and
bullion markets. By the turn of the century they were
buying up property from affluent Bengali zamindars
and in a few selected areas, posing a potential threat to
well entrenched British commercial interests.

Besides their shrewd business sense and acumen,
families like the Birlas gave Bengal and India the first
motor car to be manufactured in the country, the
"Ambassador" which, to quote Medha Kudasiya,
"between 1950 and 1970 enjoyed the reputation of
being the Indian Warhorse". Uncharitable descriptions
of the "Ambassador" by writers like Shashi Tharoor
notwithstanding (he felt it had "a steering mechanism
with the subtlety of an oxcart, guzzled gas like a sheikh
and shook like a guzzler") it was based entirely and
faithfully on the Morris prototype popular in England
around this time. Likewise their contribution to
education was not inconsiderable. Apart from primary
education in Rajasthan, the family supported instiutions
for higher education notably in Pilani, Delhi and in
Bengal, an Agricultural College and hostel. Calcutta
also benefitted by way of a Planetarium, a Museum of
Science and Technology, Hospitals and Educational
Institutions for women. Another notable contribution
by the family were the temples they built all over India.
Many were modelled on classical Hindu shrines and

were outstanding examples of indigenous architectural styles. In Calcutta the most prominent among these was the Birla Temple on Gurusaday Dutt Road. The Marwaris also set up local clubs and 'vyamshalas', which besides promoting a culture of physical fitness also donated generously to provide flood relief in Darbhanga and Burdwan.

Perhaps the least known contribution by the Marwaris, and by G.D. Birla in particular, was the growing involvement by a section of the community and the family, in nationalist politics culminating in "GD"'s close association with Mahatma Gandhi. When the latter visited Calcutta in 1915, there was great enthusiasm among the young men of Bara Bazar who decided to accord a rousing welcome to the Mahatma. When his train steamed into Howrah station, Gandhiji was met by these people who seated him on a traditional "Rath", hauled not by animals, but by the young men themselves, across the Pontoon bridge in existence at the time, all the way to Bara Bazar. Among the twenty who pulled the chariot was Ghanshyamdas Birla. His subsequent deep involvement in India's Freedom Struggle (including the issue of a warrant of arrest by the British in the Rodda Conspiracy case and his going underground until that threat was removed) has been recorded by all his biographers.

My own attitude to work was, I suspect, conditioned by a Western type education which emphasised that it was a kind of prayer—all types of work, not excluding the manual variety—and the recognition of the dignity of labour, which blurred divisions based on caste. We grew up with mottos like "Laborare est Orare (To work is to pray) or "Labore et Constantia" (Work and Resolution) and similar sounding mottos. This also impacted my religious and spiritual education in a way. Although my brother and I both attended Christian Missionary schools, we did not allow ourselves to be proselytised. Indeed, the scientific temper of that education helped to clarify my own thoughts about the creation and destiny of man, much beyond the iconography and myths which seemed to dominate Hindu religious ideas. I began to question the stark differences between Christian worship and our own and revelled in the freedom to ask, without being bullied into accepting a largely unexplained set of beliefs and rituals.

*   *   *

I never read History at school because it seemed kind of tiresome and so opted for French. The interest blosssomed after joining St Xavier's College, under the tutelage of Father Schepers, who literally brought ancient Sparta and the Peloponnesian War to life in class. In 1954 I transferred to Calcutta's Presidency College, famed for its great teachers like Prof Susobhan Chandra Sarkar, Prof. Tarak Sen and others. The College had already opened its doors to a large number of women students but their presence was regarded as something of a distraction and "free mixing" drew the usual round of taunts and taboos. Presidency College was an institution with an anti Imperialist flavour and tradition, but ironically, the ability to communicate and articulate fluently in English was regarded then, as it is now, as a mark of academic proficiency. It was something of a coincidence, I suppose, that this is where I met with my future wife disregarding the reigning canons of morality and priggish behaviour.

To belong to the Presidency College of the fifties was, as it is even now, to belong to an all pervading culture which was in some ways as formal and stylised as any. It was the culture of a so called intellectual 'elite' which had somehow lost its moorings. As the College prided itself on its stringent levels of admission, many students failed to qualify. Among the fortunate few who did, several came from the districts having graduated from government schools or from private secondary schools under the West Bengal Board. There was a dramatic variation in standards with some schools offering moderately satisfactory qualifications and others offering awards barely worth the paper they were written on. This not only affected attitudes to issues like work, marriage and religion but also created subtle shades of distinction among the students themselves. In the hierarchy of specialisation were groups of scholars, aesthetes (artists, musicians, poets etal) sportsmen (some of whom later became scholars) and of course the large body of 'ordinary' students, who, for a better description could be termed the 'apathetic mass.' Some of my colleagues had joined the College from their very first year at University. Others, like us, arrived later to enroll in the B.A./B.Sc. Honours courses.

Nowhere was the Bengali penchant for intellectual sophistry more in evidence than within the four walls of the College or the adjoining Coffee House across the road from Presidency College. The prevailing political philosophy was Marxism and the Marxist interpretation of history. This particular ethic—the middle class Marxist view of the working class—contained several errors. The middle class gentleman pities the debased worker, whose faults he sees as almost entirely the result of the grinding system which controls him. He admires the remnants of the 'noble savage' whom he wishes to restore by recourse to revolution and by drastically altering the means of production and distribution—a theory which is as impractical as it is historically inaccurate. Other topics for discussion ranged from the 'Pause' in Beethoven to the Radical Humanism of M.N. Roy. There were hair splitting arguments on Pablo Neruda and Napoleon's infidelities, none of which had any bearing on our studies. People who led or initiated these discussions, spared no time in convincing us of their Left Wing intellectual pretensions. However they all ended up as robust members of the Establishment. Far removed from Presidency's ivory towers, I happened, many years later, to ask my chauffeur if he understood the meaning of Marxism or indeed the relevance of the Left as a political force. Not unexpectedly his response was startling. He said his family only voted Communist because they were coerced into doing so by threats of brute violence. Another of Gunter Grass's "fresh young blossoms", a bright young woman in her 30s and a graduate of Jadavpur University said she always voted for the Communists because the rest of her family did so and because their "philosophy" was appealing.

Many of my contemporaries still regard the time they spent at Presidency as their "finest hour". The Guru Shishya Parampara was still in evidence at the time.

Our teachers took a genuine interest in everything we did and were delighted to guide us if we had problems, including time outside college hours without charging a fee. They lived modestly but encouraged their students to visit them at home as frequently as required. There were no strings attached. For me, some of the glamour wore off after I went abroad for higher studies, not because of any disillusionment with those kindly faces but because the whole tutorial system there was more formal and geared to generating new skills. The role of a tutor at an institution like the London School of Economics for example, was to be available to promote the student's academic and personal well being. Mine, a formidable looking lady by the name of Alice Carter was responsible for a small group of about 10 students. We met once or twice each week for discussions which did not form part of the the scheduled teaching programme and were occasions for monitoring rather than instruction. These sessions took place on a scheduled basis for group sessions and by appointment for individual contact. We were instructed never to take anything at face value, not even prescribed texts, and to search instead for opposing viewpoints through articles in scholarly journals, periodicals and other books. One of Mrs Carter's first observations about an essay I wrote on the causes of the French Revolution was a mild admonishment. She wanted to know if I was an Economic Determinist in disguise! It was of course a censure of the Marxist interpretation of history with which we were brainstormed at home. My knowledge of French helped because one of the papers for my degree included a working knowledge of at least two modern European languages, in this case, French and

Italian. Lectures were more standard but different again from the ones to which were accustomed. They were not obligatory and you only went to them if you felt the lecturer might have something new to say on the subject. Overall and in retrospect, the experience was valuable.

Although I was less of a Presidency College fan than some others, this was also as I have said before, a time when I entered a new phase of my life. I fell in love. This obsession with the object of my desire fortunately did not affect my studies but continued throughout my academic life into adulthood. The other meaningful development that occurred at this time were a few long lasting friendships which have continued until the present. They include Sabyasachi Bhattacharya, who taught for several years at the Jawaharlal Nehru University and was later nominated to the Viswabharati University in Shantiniketan as Vice Chancellor besides being elected Chairman of the Indian Council for Historical Research. His father, Prof. Nirmal Bhattacharya was Professor of Political Science at the Scottich Church College and the University of Calcutta. He joined politics and ended life as a Congress MLC in the Bidhan Roy government. Coincidentally, Sabyasachi's daughter Ashidhara was to marry our older boy, Aditya, many years later, Saugata Prasad Mukherjee's father Prof. Bimala Prasad Mukherjee was also in the academic profession. A childhood friend of Sabyasachi, Saugata was another colleague in the history department who became a member of our core group. Saugata joined the West Bengal Gazeteers Unit and also taught for a time at JNU before joining the Centre for

Social Studies in Calcutta. Yet another member of the group was Tirthankar Bose. His father Prof. Amalendu Bose taught English at the University and Tirthankar too followed in his father's footsteps. He also married his college sweetheart. After a B. Litt from Oxford on a Commonwealth Scholarship, Tirthankar taught for a while at Kalyani and Burdwan Universities before taking up an assignment at Saugor University, Udaipur. He finally emigrated to Canada. All of us, including Arup, lost touch with the fifth member of our group Jyoti Prakash Sil another bright young lad who joined the Bengal Chamber of Commerce and Industry and eventually rose to be its Secretary. We met everyday in class and during off periods, wandered off to the Coffee House across the road,. A landmark institution in the College Street area, the place was frequented by intellectuals, artists, journalists and students alike and has remained unchanged even after several decades. Sometimes in the evenings we would congregate at Sabyasachi's house on Ashwini Dutt Road with the sole purpose of a walk round the Lakes (now known as Rabindra Sarobar), and the added attraction of street food, notably the ubiquitous "phuchka". It suited my romantic inclinations at this time to start lessons in Rabindrasangeet. Chinmoy Chatterjee, a rising star in Calcutta's musical firmament had recently been inducted into the family circle. With his good looks, Chinmoy was very popular with the ladies. He was also a senior AIR artiste and had a distinctive melodic style. We were delighted when he agreed to take Tirthankar and me under his wing as students. Tirthankar was undoubtedly the better performer. My reward was getting to know Rabindranath a little better.

*   *   *

I took to learning the sarod after we were married. Thanks to my mother who played the sitar, I was introduced to Ustad Bahadur Khan at one of his regular practice sessions. His music room, crowded with portraits of his gurus, but more importantly of the Hindu Goddesses, Saraswati and Kali, was itself an education. Bahadurda as we learnt to address him, was a remarkable individual. Hailing from Commilla, now in Bangladesh, he came from a family of *Dhakis,* famous all over Bengal for their drumming at community Durga pujas, who converted to Islam. His father, Ayet Ali Khan was not only a sarod player but an instrument maker who modified the sarod as we know it today by adding additional strings and altering the shape of the drum to increase the depth and tonality of the instrument. Indeed, Hemendra Chandra Sen, the well known sarod craftsman of Calcutta and regarded by many classical instrumentalists as India's Antonio Stradivari, learnt his skills from Bahadur Khan's father. His first cousin was none other than the famous Ali Akbar Khan himself. They were both brilliant musicians. A section of Calcutta's musical cognoscenti felt that Bahadur Khan had the edge over his famous cousin. They were both tutored by the great maestro Ustad Allauddin Khan as was Pandit Ravishankar, but the sibling rivalry grew into something more disagreeable as their musical careers took off. For lack of effective public relations, Bahadur was left by the wayside while Ali Akbar moved on, ultimately to become an international celebrity. Bahadur Khan's two roomed apartment on Palm Avenue continued to reverberate to some of the most divine sarod music I have ever heard. His "Kausi Kanara" and "Umavati" are just two of the ragas I recall that dreams are made of. He dedicated his brief life to the sarod, an instrument of deep resonance and great beauty, which he treated with reverential care. In turn, it responded by strumming memories into the heart with each stroke of an 'Alap' while its rich swirling sounds reproduced 'Gats'set to incredible metres and time cycles. In short, Bahadur Khan's playing left the impress of exquisite melody combined with a filigree of intellectual and emotive improvisations rarely found in a performing artist. Bahadur Khan died due to excessive drinking. His music survives in a few tapes and audio cassettes and in the low budget films of Ritwik Ghatak an avant garde film maker of the Calcutta of that time. We lost touch with the Ustad soon afterwards as my job required me to move out of Calcutta, but his greatest gifts to me were the love of the sarod and my own instrument, fashioned under his personal supervision by Hemen Sen himself.

This account of my musical education would remain incomplete if I did not mention three other teachers, namely, Anil Mullick and Sridhar Krishnamoorthy in Chennai and Ratnakar Vyas in Bombay. All three were influenced by the Maihar gharana and were performers at different levels. Anil Mullick taught me to identify the various stages of raag devlopment, from the Alap, Jor and Jhala to the Vilambit, Madhya laya and Drut gat including various improvisations each with their formulas, not dissimilar to arithmetical and geometric progressions. I learnt to distinguish subtle variations in stroking and arrangements of notes the intervals between them and specific raag characteristics Anil Mullick was no great performer. Teaching was his livelihood and when he got married he needed to move back to his native Bengal where the opportunities to pursue his profession were greater. My next teacher, Sridhar Krishnamoorthy, then a young man in his twenties, now lives in Paris where he has a school and numerous foreign men and women disciples. Sridhar never spoke about his father but he came from a well known musical family of Tanjore and started taking lessons in Karnatic music at the age of 5 from his mother. At 10 he came under the tutelage of Ustad Zia Mohiuddeen Dagar, the great Been maestro, from whom Sridhar had his first music lessons in Hindustani music. By training therefore he was also a follower of the Maihar tradition. Sridhar's great friend, much older than himself was a mridangam player named Moorthy better known to his compatriots as N.V. Moorthy. An expert on the tabla tarang, Mr Moorthy played the mridangam and the tabla with equal dexterity, except that he never forgot the teachings of his guru Vidwan Palghat Mani Iyer and treated the 'bayan' like a mridangam slapping it flat with his left hand without producing any of its characteristic modulations. However his 'matra' calculations were faultless. From Moorthy's vast store of Karnatic 'talas' I learnt the intricacies of rhythm, metres and time cycles including the all important concept of strong and weak beats. Sridhar often matched the Hindustani and Carnatic drum syllables on his sarod to illustrate how certain types of improvisations could be created without sacrificing the melodic line. Both were proud that they had transcended local barriers to travel abroad on concert tours.

Around this time, I was fortunate to be invited by the British Council in Madras to deliver two lectures on Hindustani Classical music. I had never spoken in public before and was nervous. Finally a friend reassured me that the best way to get over my "nerves" was to counsel myself into believing that no one in the audience was likely to know more about the subject than I. It seemed to work at the time but I would not bet on it! Later, I was selected by the Max Mueller Bhavan to represent them at an East West Musical Encounter in Pune. The "Encounter" which began with a recital by Ustad Imrat Khan contained many items of interest for afficionados and experts alike, such as talks and lectures by eminent German and Indian exponents, a Western music concert by a well known Chamber Music Group from Bombay playing selections from Haydn, Beethoven and Mozart and a counter performance by Prof Manfred Junius from Munich of the Raag Shyam Kalyan on the surbahar. It ended with a dinner hosted by the Director of the Max Mueller Bhavan, Pune at his house on Boat Club Road.

The other memorable musical experience of this period was an evening Amita and I spent with our friends V.P. and Kalpagam Raman at their house in Mylapore. "VP" was a high flying solicitor but it was said of him that if he quit law and took to playing serious (Karnatic) classical music on the violin he could compete with the best. His wife was a talented vocalist. We were invited to meet Ramnad Krishnan one of South India's rising classical vocalists in the sixties. The reason why the evening turned out to be so extraordinary was our initiation that evening into classical Karnatic music. Apart from Ramnad Krishnan's own mellifluous voice the South Indian raga system is different from ours and like Rabindrasangeet relies to a great extent on its lyrics (kritis), composed in the main by stalwarts like Thyagaraja, Shyama Shastri and Dikshitar. The lyrics have all been carefully transliterated and translated, so that listening becomes pure enjoyment. Karnatic ragas are microcosms of their Hindustani counterparts, consisting of all the basics, but briefer in their development. "VP" introduced us to a remarkable collection of Thyagaraja's "kritis" in a book by that name which even today adorns my book shelf.

I met Shri Ratnakar Vyas through my friend, Prafulla Dahanukar when we moved from Chennai to Bombay in 1971. Prafulla is one of the country's leading painters. She married a scion of the Dahanukar family who own a mansion on Bombay's exclusive Cumballa Hill on a street named after the family. When she was not painting, Prafulla was totally engrossed in vocal classical music. To her, Bhimsen Joshi, Kishori Amonkar, Veena Sahasrabuddhe, Padma Talwalkar, Arati Anklikar and many others were household names. We served together for a time on the Committee of the Bade Ghulam Ali Yaadgar Sabha of which she was the Secretary. This was a Registered Public Charitable Trust named after one of the country's greatest vocalists who died in penury. The Trust was established to raise funds for such artistes. Related to the eminent vocalist, C.R.Vyas, Ratnakar lived in a small tenement in the Municipal Colony adjoining Shivsagar Estate in Worli by virtue of his wife's employment in a Municipal school. She was herself a Sangeet Visharad from the Marris School of Music in Lucknow but never flaunted this qualification.

Totally devoted to her husband and his music, she was content to accompany him on the tanpura at public concerts. Ratnakar was a simple soul. He never mentioned money and I was careful to lay whatever I could afford, at his feet, each time we met for a lesson. This went on for a couple of years until he was offered a teaching assignment with the Bharatiya Vidya Bhavan in London. He returned sick and broken. London had not agreed with him. He felt lonely, miserable and homesick. Our lessons became more and more infrequent and finally when I left for Calcutta to be at my father's bedside when he died, they ended. Ratnakar was a remarkable man and a great human being. During a particularly turbulent period of my life, he stood by my side and threw his home open not only for free music lessons but for any counsel or help I might want. He also introduced us to an extraordinary person—a clairvoyant, Pandit Kashinath Durve Shastri, who predicted, with pin point accuracy, virtually everything (mostly the good things) that came to fruition over the next few years. I was grateful to Ratnakar for his largesse, his commitment to his students but above all, for his love and compassion. When I returned to Bombay after an absence of two years, Ratnakar was gone. He had moved out of his little apartment with his wife and daughter, after his wife retired from service and nobody in the Colony seemed to know their whereabouts except that they had shifted to the city's northern suburbs to an undisclosed address. We never met after that.

I regret I did not, due to my own laziness, pursue the study of the sarod as assiduously as I might have done. I confess I played truant when it came to rigorous practice. However, my long association with classical Indian music gave me a window to an incredible world of musicians and performers whose creativity often surpassed traditional foundations and gave me an insight into an extraordinarily complex musical system which had survived for centuries. We were fortunate that some of the country's finest musicians were gracious enough to perform at home. They included Ustad Amjad Ali Khan, Ustad Alla Rakha and his illustrious son Zakir, Ustad Aslam Khan, Ustad Munnawar Ali Khan, Ustad Asad Ali Khan and Ustad Shamim Ahmed. I have never been attracted to the modern concept of fusion between Eastern and Western musical idioms. The dissimilarities are far more than the similarities. "Harmonisation" in the strictly Western sense for example, would require many aspects of Indian music to be sacrificed, among them subtlety of melody, complexities of rhythm and the purity of intervals between notes. Ravishankar attempted it with the London Philharmonic conducted by Andre Previn but the combination sounded strangely unfamiliar. Before he died, the guru himself admitted that fusion could only lead to confusion. Experiments have been made to combine classical Indian music with Western style opera and ballet, but here too there are obvious limitations. However within the sub continent there have been many welcome improvisations, such as the introduction of several South Indian Ragas into the more Persianised North Indian variety or the Sawal Jawab, the dialogue between the sitar and the tabla, borrowed from the Tal Vadya Kacheri of South India The Jugalbandi or duet between two instrumentalists was also an innovation when it was first introduced.

Today it is an accepted technique among North Indian musicians.

*   *   *

The repressed ambience of the man woman relationship in India is more palpable in Eastern than in Western India. Even the heroines of Bankim Chandra, Rabindranath and Sarat Chandra—names like Tilottoma and Ayesha (Durgeshnandini),Kapalkundala and Padmabati (Kapalkundala), Prafulla (Debi Choudhurani), Hoimonti, Binodini(Binodini), Mrinmoyee(Samapti), Bimla (Ghare Baire), Labanya (Shesher Kobita), Lalita (Parineeta), Parvati and Chandramukhi (Devdas), Rajlakshmi (Srikanta) and Savitri(Charitraheen) to mention just a few, were examples of varying degrees of emancipation, courage, restraint and sacrifice within the marital bonds. Relationships outside marriage were regarded as unlawful and/or suggested by inference. Pitted against these women, Bengali men emerged as weak and indecisive characters. Inevitably though, it was the male ego that needed to be satisfied and placated. Sex was always under wraps. It was considered indecent and improper to discuss the topic in print. Rabindranath's songs too are full of inuendos about the physical aspects of romantic love. This is not to deny the existence of the sexual factor in Bengali homes. Stories of incest and physical intimacy between consenting adults are not unknown. However, until recently, Bengali novelists and film makers—even the great Satyajit Ray himself—graciously and politely skirted the issue. It is for consideration to what extent and for how long, these attitudes and postures will continue to influence contemporary Bengali middle class morality and behaviour. We all know that among the lower echelons of Bengali society the rules are more lax and that the younger generation is striving to strike out on its own

Most Bengali males are pampered silly by their mothers sisters and wives. Those that aren't adopt postures bordering on the ridiculous. With the breakup of joint families pre arranged marriages which in the past signifed more a union of families than of two individuals are giving way to personal choice. However, the man/ woman equation is still somewhat nebulous. Indian philosophy recognises three models (a) the Brahma Maya model which denies any status to women (b) the Purusa Prakriti model which recognises a woman's independent existence and (c) the Siva Shakti model in which woman is respected. Unfortunately, these postulates are freely interpreted in society to mean different things at different times to suit a patriarchal system which is essentially male dominated. Most middle class homes across the country follow this pattern with the result that in polite company it is inappropriate to talk about sexual freedom, let alone the explicits. What emerges is a sterile picture of matrimony in which the partners are seemingly oblivious of each other's presence in public but fully aware of the need to fulfill one's obligations to the other including the sacrifice of one's personal happiness, in private. Concepts like premarital or post marital relationships are strictly taboo and spoken about in whispers. This largely Victorian image of marriage was promoted in the 19th and 20th centuries through the literature of the period.

According to newspaper reports, Bengal has a higher percentage of literacy among women than the national average. However it ranks amongst the lowest when it comes to autonomy enjoyed by them in marriage. The survey included parameters like the power to take decisions about her own health, household purchases and freedom to visit her family/relatives. At another workshop on Census and the National Health Survey conducted in 2011 it was reported that in rural areas, "the average homemaker in Bengal spends two hours daily fetching water and six hours a week collecting firewood." It has been estimated and indeed we know at first hand, that toilet facilities for women in rural and urban areas are deplorable. This is a state which which got its first woman Chief Minister six and a half decades after independence, and by contrast, stands mute witness to the rising violence against women. Indeed, according to the National Crime Records Bureau, the rate of growth in crime against women in the state, now outstrips the national average! The list covers domestic violence, suicide on account of dowry, rape and molestation.

On balance, I think, Bengali women are far more acceptable than their male counterparts. They are sagacious, compassionate, delicate, discreet and courageous to name only a few qualities—qualities which, in a different context, Vatsayana has described as "soft and sweet in speech, full of love and tender in their bodies." The patriarchal system notwithstanding, I can think of several outstanding examples where these "soft spoken women, full of love and tender in their bodies" have exhibited qualities which would put any man to shame. In the depths of rural Bengal where my wife and I have had the privilege of working, we have met women battered and bruised by their husbands who have built up their own incomes to support families of four and five children. One such home we visited consisted of a family of seven including the husband's parents. They subsisted on rice and boiled potatoes In another, the woman of the house traded her personal possessions to a gang of robbers for a sewing machine she had purchased a few weeks ago on the plea that it was her only source of income. We have come across sexual abuse and children who are visually, mentally or physically challenged and we have met families where the mother's lack of a formal education vis-à-vis other members of the household, is her biggest handicap. Yet, but for these mothers, the bottom would be knocked out of our social fabric.

I came across a close parallel to the man woman relationship in traditional Indian society after reading Elizabeth Gilbert's description of the Hmong women of South Viet Nam. Here was a community where men and women led separate lives. In the author's own words, "Yes you have a spouse. Yes you have sex with that spouse. Yes, your fortunes are tied together. Yes there might very well be love. But aside from that, men's and women's lives are quite firmly separated into the divided realms of their gender-specific tasks. Men work and socialise with other men; women work and socialise with other women." She goes on to say "If you are a Hmong woman, you don't necessarily expect your husband to be your best friend, your most intimate confidante, your emotional adviser, your intellectual equal, your comfort in times of sorrow. Hmong women, instead, get that emotional nourishment from other women—from sisters, aunts, mothers and grandmothers." This is, of course, almost identical to the situation which exists in our own society and very different from the Western concept of the man woman relationship in a nuclear society, both in and out of marriage, where the spouse/ boyfriend/girlfriend becomes the sole repository of the other's trust.

Fortunately or unfortunately—I am not quite sure which—women and womens' issues appear to be changing. Young urban Indian women are more assertive, independent and career minded. Thanks to globalisation, they now have many more career options, dress differently, are acutely aware of their sexuality and amenable, more than ever before, to remain single for extended periods. Marriage and/or raising a family are quite definitely not on their list of priorities. They are learning to communicate, to be self sufficient, secure and confident. They are into free relationsihps, where fidelity and commitment are the only criteria and where they are personally accountable for their growth and responsibilities.

*   *   *

I have always been partial to women with courage and spirit. Both my wife and my mother came from Bengal. Neither corresponded to the stereotypical image of the Indian woman and were, I believe in advance of their time. I first saw Amita at a function to celebrate the Centenary of my future college. She was on stage with a group of fellow students preparing to sing a collection of Tagore songs which, by convention, would signal the formal commencement of the main function. It was a moment of discovery. My world suddenly narrowed down to a face—a rather beautiful face which, at that particular moment in time, I thought was frankly, without parallel. Not a word was exchanged and certainly Amita was unaware of my presence in the audience. It was one of those rare coincidences in life which guides our destinies and shapes future events. In this case that sighting was to impact both of us for the rest of our lives. Coming from a bastion of Kolkata's Kayastha families Amita completed her Masters and went on to a Ph.d from Oxford on a Commonwealth Scholarship, unchaperoned and entirely on her own. Her academic achievements had already made her something of a celebrity in those years. After we were married, Amita taught briefly at Calcutta University and subsequently at two womens' colleges in Madras and Bombay where my work took me. She joined the Nehru Centre, Mumbai as Senior Research Officerwhere she spent the next 20 years. She visited Britain on a British Council Visitorship in 1985 and again on a Nuffield Fellowship in 1988 for three months. On the second occasion, she was attached to the Commonwealth Institute in London to contribute to its redevelopment plans and to study new ideas and concepts on museum design and historical displays. British museum technology had undergone revolutionary changes in terms of sites, audio visual effects and three dimensional models. One of the reasons which prompted her to study these displays was to try and incorporate a few ideas for the permanent exhibition on India's history

"The Discovery of India," spanning over 5000 years, which she was coordinating at the Nehru Centre. The exhibition was finally inaugurated by the President of India in 1994. In her final years at the Nehru Centre that institution made an exception and offered her an apartment on the premises so that she could continue with her work at the Centre. It was a very happy coincidence for us as it enabled Amita to carry on working even after my corporate innings ended and for both our boys, Pramit in particular, to complete their initial round of studies at University. Pramit secured a First Class Honours Degree in Economics from Bombay University and Aditya, far removed from Bombay at the time and at a different level, qualified to enter the Ph.d. programme in Chemical Engineering at Carnegie Mellon in the US after successfully completing his B.Sc. and M.Sc. degrees from the Universities of New Hampshire and West Virginia respectively.

Amita was a true blue Bengali if ever there was one. As was customary at the time, she was born in her maternal grandfather's apartment just off Maddox Square on 13 Earl Street. She grew up in her ancestral home in School Row annd later went to school at St John's Diocesan, a Protestant school for girls with a pronounced Indian bias from the family's new home on 1, Chowringhee Terrace. Amita distinguished herself by standing First among women students at the State's first School Final Examination. Her scholastic achievements enabled her to qualify for admission to Calcutta's prestigeous Presidency College, which, apart from being singled out as an institution for academic excellence was also associated with India's National movement. Amita obtained first a Bachelor's and then a Master's Degree in History with First Class Honours. She was an accomplished Rabindrasangeet singer from 'Gitabitan' having trained under masters like Niharbindu Sen and Sm. Kanak Biswas. She could have qualified for a career on stage if she wished. Amita's father, Jatindra Mohan was one of eight brothers and sisters and family gatherings in the house on School Row were part of an ongoing patriarchal tradition. Bengal and its cultural ethos ran in Amita's blood. Throughout her stay at Oxford University she never wore anything but a sari and never consciously or unconsciously acquired an "Oxford accent." Amita's paternal grandmother was a regal and very good looking woman. Born into a family of traditional landowners, the Roychowdhurys of Taki-Sodepur, Golapbashini as she was called, was, to all intents and purposes, the mistress of the household in School Row. I have a feeling Amita admired her grandmother sufficiently to model herself on the lady. Her paternal grandfather, Biraj Mohan, migrated from Khulna in East Bengal (now Bangladesh). He too belonged to a landowning family and was a well known lawyer of his day. Biraj Mohan was closely associated with one of Calcutta's eminent nationalist families—the family of Sir Ashutosh and Shyamaprosad Mookherjee. Sir Ashutosh was a prominent educationist who helped set up Calcutta's Law College. His son Shyamaprosad was a Minister in Nehru's first Cabinet and founded the Hindu Mahasabha. His grandson, Chittatosh, was in turn Chief Justice of the Calcutta and Madras High courts and acting Governor of Maharashtra for a brief period. In pre Independence India, the male members of the Mookherjee and Majumdar families were educated

in Bhowanipore's Mitra Institution, a nationalist school
founded as an alternative to the more Westernised
Christian missionary schools.

Amita's father's decision to move out of the School
Row house with his family to their new home on
Chowringhee Terrace was the first break with tradition,
creating ripples among the other members of the
Majumdar clan. Even the location of the house, situated
as it was in the peripheries of White Town, was suspect.
The architect, Bhupati Chowdhury built it in the Art
Nouveau /Art Deco style, a style which was popular
and fashionable among affluent families in the 30s of
the last century. Its main attractions were the lavish
use of Italian marble and modern bathrooms with
Western style showers, bathtubs and mirrors. One of
the bathrooms, with a mermaid inlaid in mosaic on the
wall, even sported a bidet. An unsuspecting visitor was
hit on the face by a jet of water when he accidentlally
turned on one of the taps! The house on Chowringhee
Terrace became a focus of attention when Amita's father
converted the ground floor into an exhibition gallery
which he let out free of cost for art and photographic
exhibitions. There were no art galleries in Calcutta
at the time and the facility at Chowringhee Terrace
not only served as a succour to struggling painters
and photograhers but is remembered even today as an
epic landmark in the city. The second was his decision
to send his daughter to a coeducational college; the
third, when he permitted her to travel overseas on a
scholarship and the last, albeit reluctantly, to let her
marry the man of her choice. In the context of his time,
Mr Jatindra Mohan Majumdar was, in many ways, a

Renaissance person. Gregarious and outgoing, he had a large circle of friends and was very active in Calcutta's intellectual and social circles. Amita was deeply attached to her family and always dreamt of returning to the city where she was born.

My mother's world was entirely different. She grew up in the moffusil towns of Faridpur and Rangpur (now in Bangladesh). As an imaginative and creative child given to singing, painting and writing she spent most of her time in the company of nature, including birds and flowers. As the younger of two siblings who was decidedly less flashy, she led a protected and unexciting kind of life with her parents and was ready for marriage when she was only sixteen and totally unprepared. In many ways her marriage to my father was an accident. My grandparents who were looking for a suitable groom for my mother's older sister invited my father home to meet his prospective bride. They were dazzled by his brilliance and good looks, not to speak of his service credentials. However when the meeting finally took place, my father's gaze quickly shifted from my aunt to her shy younger sister whose personality and looks appealed to him more than his intended prospective. Their subsequent marriage proved to be hard work for both of them. My father married against his father's wishes—he had his own reasons for doing so—and the resultant animosity between the two, lasted a lifetime. My mother needed to adjust not only to the kind of sophistications required by the colonial ruling society of the time in which my father moved, but with the passing years, to many of my father's moods and idiosyncracies. Temperamentally, they were very different. My father, an Economist, understood his subject better than the fine arts. Although he was very supportive of my mother, his personal involvement was lacking. Moreover, his frequent transfers to and from the Districts/Calcutta/Delhi were major upheavals which Mother had to deal with virtually singlehandedly. He was impatient, quick tempered and intolerant of people. She was highly sensitive, compassionate and wise. In their early years, when they were posted in the districts, my mother trained herself to deal with domestic issues,including the management of staff, parenting and rearing children. In the absence of any kind of entertainment, she was compelled to virtually carve out her own interests. She sang, played the sitar and the esraj, sewed, knitted, and embroidered and like many educated women of her day, was a voracious reader. Indeed, at times, she would startle us by her views on contemporary issues and values. Despite prolonged bouts of ill health she found time to graduate first from the Government College of Art in Kolkata and subsequently, from Kolkata's City College with a Bachelor of Arts degree. Many years later, she held solo exhibitions of her paintings in India and abroad, and during two arduous years when she battled for survival with a diseased thyroid she managed to qualify for a diploma in textile designing from the Central School of Art in London. Back home, she worked for the Khadi and Handloom Industries Board, Government of India, where her designs were widely exhibited and sold. Her husband's service notwithstanding, my Mother joined the group that joined Mahatma Gandhi to tour the riot torn villages of Noakhali, after the Riots of 1946-'47 where she met many co-sympathisers and made numerous friendships which were to last a lifetime. My earliest memories of my mother were those of a great cook, hostess, nurse and playmate rolled into one.

My mother was no classic beauty, but she always dressed well enough to make eyes turn. Even a homespun plain white cotton sari appeared sophisticated, as it fell in graceful folds round her ankles. She was the kind of woman Audrey Hepburn once described as being known not by the clothes she wore or by the figure she carried or the way she combed her hair (although she had all three in good measure) but by her eyes, which were full of love and caring. I think as children we were mesmerised by those eyes. There was something in her personality—empathy, dignity and restraint, call it by any name you wish—that attracted men and women alike to seek her friendship. As children, I cannot remember a single day when my mother screamed at us, abused, or spanked us. It was a lesson in model parenting if ever there was one.

Many people have asked me what it was that drew Amita and I together. One reason, I suspect, was that my reactions to people and situations were very different—almost unconventional—by comparison to the men she grew up with. I was and still am, open to a wide variety of opinions, I practised what I preached and if nothing else, kept Amita entertained with anecdotes and postures which she must have found amusing. Amita, had a rainbow deep down in her heart which I sensed would sustain us throughout life. Barring these observations, it did not take me long to discover that despite the outward shackles of convention, she was a woman with a free will. This was very important to someone with my upbringing and demands. No woman in the Majumdar family had ever married a man of her choice. No woman married or unmarried had stepped out of the family to carve out a career, much less to travel abroad alone. No man or woman in the family had ever tasted beef. None had ever hitch hiked across Europe in a sari or any other outfit and of course no member of the family ever matched her scholastic achievements. As a Commonwealth scholar in England, there were other privileges like shaking the hand of India's first Prime Minister, Jawaharlal Nehru or attending a Guildhall Dinner presided by Harold Macmillan and meeting members of the British royal family—like the Queen (when she came to Oxford to inaugurate the L.M.H. Library) and Princess Margaret (at a reception to meet Commonwealth Scholars)—at sufficiently close quarters to exchange a few words. Amita has been my best friend, and worst critic, but there were significant differences in our responses to people and situations. Like most young couples we started out by doing things together. However there were areas of interest we could never share. Our marriage was a matter of mutual trust, of uncharted and exciting possibilities combined with a degree of cautious optimism. It was a partnership which needed to be carefully nurtured and evaluated against each one's strengths and weaknesses. We had our share of disagreements and faced situations which would have left many others totally broken. At times like these we drew on our mutual reserves to be able to concentrate on the positives and to convince ourselves just how much we needed and meant to each other. On occasions when faith, courage and tenacity were the only options to fight misfortune, we tried to rise beyond the immediate circumstances and to look for alternatives beyond the obvious, to survive. Such eventualities were certainly not part of our dreams when we were courting. I think both of us gave up a little of ourselves to make the marriage work, although I suspect Amita sacrificed more than I did. She has been my guardian angel, my protector and trustee in all moments of crisis. On the bookshelf in my study at Jubilee Park is a black and white portrait of Amita on her sixth birthday. It was taken by Shambhu Saha a well known photographer of that time in the house at Chowringhee Terrace. I never tire of looking at it because Shambhu Babu captured the whole personality of his subject in that instant—the childish innocence of those eyes and the smile which has captivated me ever since we met.

Having said that, and at the risk of sounding slightly facetious, I cannot honestly say I was not susceptible to attentions by women beyond immediate family. Indeed, there was a time when there was nothing nicer than to be attractive to a pretty young woman to boost my male ego, especially where the bestower was personable and radiant in a way that appealed to my senses. I have been mistaken on and off for a film star and a celebrity musician, complimented for my "performance" at the previous night's concert; on intimate physical attributes I never really possessed; even openly solicited and propositioned. It was only possible to treat these encounters without being too defensive and not to deny the obvious, but I would have been poorer without them. They do not reflect my views on all women and I confess I am still vulnerable.

So when a gorgeous niece chooses to describe me as her "soulmate" or when another says I am a person with "style" I crave indulgence and some good humoured acceptance. Equally, if someone were to ask if I still felt disposed to chasing women, I would say as Bob Hope once did, "only downhill!" I choose to describe this interest as "empathy" rather than a "weakness" for the opposite sex. Considering that a few women,—not all of the glamorous variety—have played pivotal roles in the troughs and peaks of my life, I think it difficult for any outsider to pass judgement on a relationship. Life goes by with its successes and challenges and this puts stresses on all of us, as we change and grow as persons.

*   *   *

Having lived outside Calcutta for well over 30 years, most of it over the course of my working life—in Bombay (Mumbai)—friends and relatives were curious to discover how we would readjust to living in Calcutta. The stark differences between the two cities were palpable. So were people behaviour and work ethics. When we moved there in early 1971 a friend confided that Bombay would teach us in two weeks what we needed to know about life in two years anywhere else in India! At the time of leaving I think I understood what those words meant. This partcular metropolis was no less unequal than most other Indian cities. Wealth, poverty and sleaze lived side by side on its pavements, but more importantly, the events I witnessed in my immediate work and social environment during the last few years of our stay, were the stuff of novels.

My own attraction to Calcutta was also, inevitably, the family property in Jubilee Park but the ties were more tenuous. My father was on transferable service and as a family we kept shuttling between Government accommodation to which my father was entitled, in Calcutta and Delhi. In fact my father bought the house in Jubilee Park from a Portuguese couple after retirement with the express purpose of sharing a portion of it with his parents who were forced out of the ancestral home in Dhaka after Partition. Unfortunately this did not happen because my grandfather passed away before the move materialised. My grandmother, a strict vegetarian, did not share our kitchen and while staying with us, had to be provided for separately. The house appealed to my mother because in many ways, it reminded her of the stately bungalows assigned to members of the Civil Service in India, only smaller. It was designed in the colonial pattern, by the well known firm of British architects, Ballardie Thompson and Matthew, typified by high ceilings, Burmah teak doors and windows, and a wide staircase with cast iron balustrades to match, with polished wooden bannisters. The floors were made of red patent stone whose distinctive granite like finish, was the pride of Bird & Co, the firm that made them popular in the thirties of the last century. Our house was a retreat from the noise and bedlam of the city, being as I have already mentioned, located in a mango grove opposite the Tollygunge Club on land that once belonged to the late Prince Gholam Mohammed Shah of the Mysore royal family. More importantly, it gave us a sense of belonging. Like the proverbial banyan, it served as a roof over our heads when we needed it most. Although I did not "belong" to Calcutta in the same way my wife did, the city was not unfamiliar terrain. I had been in and out of Calcutta throughout my childhood and growing years. I was critical of its shortcomings, but did not despair of the possibility of carving a niche for myself, even though the prospect appeared to be chaotic at the time.

Both my parents had their own individual spaces and identities—he, as an Economist and popular writer of Bengali novels, and she, as a painter and textile designer, not to mention her deep spiritual interests. My father's writing skills served him well for many years and his service credentials were formidable enough to sustain the family fortunes he died. When I lost them both within a few years of each other in the 90s, I felt that as the sole heir, I had a responsibility to manage the property and to perpetuate, in some small measure, the memories and values they cherished.

*   *   *

There were other compulsions. One of these was the desire to break away from the people, the thoughts and the aspirations that had occupied me for the major part of my working life. I had entered the Corporate world on the rebound, having compromised my overseas degree for a half hearted attempt at qualifying for the Civil Service. I had no love lost for either although I confess that given the circumstances, I could not have hoped for a better career than the one I was offered by the people who finally elected to have me. My terms of appointment were negotiated in England and and I have no doubt that had I continued in the corporate sector, I would probably have ended by heading the Company's Indian operations.

Corporate types, by which I mean salaried Indian executives who made their careers in the older generation of British companies, were, and I suspect still are, part of an extraordinary culture. I have already talked elsewhere of the quintessential Imperial style of functioning which was basically to segregate the rulers from the ruled and to set up postures of superiority where the natives would be beholden to their foreign masters. Here was a captive audience on whom the new rulers could, to quote Ian Baucom, "secure the boundaries of their own identities to discipline the identitities of their subjects." It was a conscious process of subjugation, involving religious beliefs, and setting up legal, administrative and social institutions where the prime motive was to create an aura of grandeur "before which the native would submit with respect and admiration to the reformation of his or her identity." These values have now been replaced by a kind of half baked local exclusivity to establish priorities and a culture of mediocrity. Company profiles and mindsets have undergone a sea change. Competition is intense and commercial considerations have taken precedence over loyalties and business ethics. In my day the choice of a corporate career in India was one of five options. You could either teach, or join the Administratve service, qualify as a Doctor, Engineer or Lawyer or go into Tea garden management, an attractive route for persons who had no wish to pursue higher studies and who liked the great outdoors. In the majority of cases there was no formal training for new recruits. Management of human resources and materials were learnt on the job very often under a senior employee who was either sceptical of Management education or just plain ignorant. All this has changed. There are many more opportunities. Management is more focussed and specialised. The numbers of job aspirants, have ballooned and there are disturbing signs in domestic and international markets, of criminal involvement and large scale fraud at the highest levels.

I tended at first to be slightly condescending about my British peers, most of whom had never been to University or had worked their way up the corporate ladder from either the drawing board or foreman level. I therefore insisted that I should be appointed on the same terms as the company's expatriate staff serving overseas especially as these positions were described as being in the "covenanted" category and commanded an extraordinary range of perquisites. The word had a special significance in India, where members of the Indian Civil Service were referred to as "covenanted officers" or officers who had agreed to serve under a covenant signed by the Secretary of State on behalf of the Crown. No such precedent was of course applicable to commercial assistants, except perhaps to define their eligibility for membership of elite British Clubs and the perquisites referred to above. These included fully furnished company accommodation, a company car, leave travel for self and wife, reimbursement of medical expenses including hospitalisation, for the executive and his family, leave travel also for the whole family and at more senior levels, unlimited entertaining, cost of soft furnishings, domestic staff, electricity and water bills. The pompous and rather affected gentleman who interviewed me had served for many years in India and was decidedly suspicious of my coloured waistcoat. I realised later that this was something of a posture. He was keen to impress me with the scope of his own authority, his knowledge of the sub continent and about service conditions in India. When I met the Head of the Company's Calcutta Branch at lunch the following week, I was convinced that British managers who had made the grade in India were by and large drawn from a group educated at what is now called a secondary modern school. A few, had, at best, completed their "O" levels. Those from the Armed forces tended to patronise the "boorish" attitudes of their colleagues and the fact that they were not quite gentlemen. However they all quickly adjusted to Indian obsequiousness by adopting postures of superiority. They were in a very different class from my associates at University and also from native Englishmen and women who had never lived and worked abroad. Our Calcutta Manager was a Scotsman with a great handlebar moustache nursed since his days with the Royal Air Force. He was slightly withdrawn but his wife displayed her origins. He never ordered anything except an omelette even at expensive restaurants, presumably to save the company from undue extravagance! On one occasion he admonished me by saying that the Company would not be responsible for my "bar bills" after he was presented with a bill for a glass of beer I had consumed at lunch while on duty. I later learnt with dismay that he was the "Burra Saab" to his Indian staff. "Never underestimate anybody in this office" another English colleague in the Company's Calcutta Branch with an Australian wife once cautioned me in a mixture of Hammersmith and Aussie accents, after I finished explaining the intricacies of an isosceles triangle! He was right in a way. Every white man in India, even a backpacker, was entitled to imagine they knew it all and revelled in the perks enjoyed two centuries ago, by East India Company officials! The Babus were an entirely different breed with great big chips on their shoulders who needed to be treated with kid gloves. I had an edge over other Indian executives because of my overseas degree but was deflected from flaunting it by a variety of subterfuges. In the end it worked to my advantage. Thanks to the Government of India's policy of Indianisation, a number of expats had to leave the country and vacancies in the higher echelons of the Company's management had to be filled by locals. I quickly rose from Junior to Senior Assistant and from Senior Assistant to Regional Manager in the time it would normally take for anyone to move up just one step. In the process, I too, learnt some valuable lessons more particularly in the area of human resource develoment and the more technical aspects of the business. I personally visited every single customer, starting from large industrial houses to bazar dealers with whom sharing cups of syrupy tea in chipped cups was part of normal courtesy. When a piece of equipment used for oil dispensing broke down, I was taught to take it apart and put it together again so that I would not be misled by professional repairers. Likewise I was inducted into detailed discussions with trade unions, civil and mechanical engineers and law firms. By the time my practical training on the job ended I was ready for a transfer of residence to Madras and a Management course at Ashridge in the UK.

Subsequently, I was picked for a senior management position in the Company's headquarters in Bombay.

During this time I travelled all over the country and the world, sometimes in company with my wife and sometimes alone, but always with the self assurance of success and the confidence that accompanies it. The view from the top echelons of management is very different from problem solving at regional level. I found that to be effective I needed to communicate better, to set examples and to avoid creating undesirable precedents. Much more emphasis was needed in planning and strategising than on day to day management of resources. I was called to represent the Division I was heading at International Conferences, coordinated and prepared 5 year rolling plans besides talking and writing about aspects of the business. Other important contributions to the company's growth prospects were to standardise service conditions across the country and to revamp the company's advertising and publicity strategies including active participation at national exhibitions and major sporting events. At one point I even made a film about the company and its products. The film was shown in Bombay's leading cinema houses! I was also offered an international assignment with a house and private swimming pool in Zimbabwe which I declined because it would interfere with my childrens' education.

Given that this was a period of transition in the company's history, there were not many Indians fit to take over from the expatriate managers who were leaving, especially as there was no consistent succession planning. Indianisation had been haphazard. This led to a policy of cross fertilisation with affiliated companies within the group with identical or similar product lines. It also led to the induction of persons who were either unfamiliar with the company's existing culture or conditions of service. Two key positions were allotted to persons in this category. They moved into Bombay from Delhi and distant Assam. Neither was familiar with the company's existing operations, its products or its culture. They moved bag and baggage into available company accommodation denying claims by existing senior management to these properties, with serious and long lasting repercussions. The transition from European to Indian management was palpable. Business ethics changed overnight, company property became individual assets and power lines and job designations recast in the name of "modernisation" to cater to the Indian penchant for grandiose titles. It was something of a culture shock to find a group of strangers who had nothing whatsoever to do with the company or its manufacturing interests, guzzling great quantities of expensive Scotch whisky as guests of the new Chief Executive or driving away in company cars because they felt they had earned the right to do so. Worse, a certain cake shop in Bombay's Taj Mahal Hotel as well as the hotel's exclusive restaurants began to be freely patronised by the CEO, his family and a close circle of friends, all at company expense.

In due course I discovered that managerial authorities were being eroded by a group of persons who were susceptible to temptation and for favours they could not disclaim. In consequence they lent themselves to participate in patently actionable ventures. Kickbacks were shared, accounting improprieties balanced by reclassifying expenses and budgets suitably padded as "operating expenses" to enable them and their cronies to spend extra money on their own lavish lifestyles. Those who differed were either held to ransom, blackmailed or simply liquidated. This culture based on the rationale that the whites were worse, was alien to my way of thinking. Judging by historical events, the conclusion was probably true. Nevertheless it took some time to shake off the "omelette" tradition contrived though it might have been, for the benefit of the company's Indian staff.

Not all Indian senior corporate executives of my generation, were exposed to my kind of apprenticeship. For the most part they played, drank hard, drove around in swank cars and adopted lifestyles to suit much inflated salaries. They were not much good at entrepreneurship or intellectual skills. A survey conducted by the Shri Ram Centre for Industrial Relations in New Delhi came to several interesting conclusions. They found for example that while most managers read newspapers and light magazines, they did not read serious journals. Half the people interviewed had never read a management related book. Forty percent of the managers did no reading either on or off the job. Finally, there was no consistent or integrated attitudes towards reading. Another study conducted by the University of Sheffield on the same subject, though more broadbased, came to the conclusion that there were urban professional groups who believed that reading was a boring activity and a waste of time. Another group of marginal readers felt that they would rather do other activities than read and only read if it was necessary. Yet another read books because they were job related and because it would give them the required skills to improve themselves. Some professionals did not deny that reading was important but did not have the time because of "work pressures".

Another breed of corporate types were those who had been propelled to managemnt positions having mastered a whole host of on-the-job skills. They were ashamed to talk about their early education or their family origins. It didn't really matter, because behind a veneer of sophistication, which corporate life inevitably demanded, their patently clumsy manners were more than familiar. Their ignorance of Western culture matched the appalling and somewhat disconcerting innocence of their own, living life as many of their compatriots seemed to do, by bread alone, combined with a few worldly attributes like a sharp instinct for self preservation and a shrewd sense of practical purpose. Indian companies needed them to work as fixers, or to create barriers. They were aggressive, or supplicatory as the occasion demanded and adept at the art of retreat. Not surprisingly they lacked finesse and were pathetic performers when it came to interacting with the opposite sex.

A section of corporate wives presented themselves as alluring mistresses. They would happily sleep around with their husband's bosses or colleagues if the situation demanded. This was particularly true in self contained company towns and campuses outside of metropolitan limits, but the urban libido, alas, was not inconsiderable.

These "Peyton Place" like situations—after a novel of that name which exposed the scandals of American sexuality in a small New England township—doubtless appealed to an ambitious breed of Indian women who considered their behaviour fashionable. They preyed on their husbands' colleagues to garner support and sometimes presented themselves as stepping stones to success. One corporate wife I knew staged a mock separation from her husband, complete with legal documents, with the sole purpose of fulfilling her sexual fantasies. Used judiciously and with discretion, these ploys could reap rich rewards. Not surprisingly, my corporate innings ended on issues of principle.

*   *   *

I got to know a little bit about rural India after quitting the corporate life and taking on an assignment as Executive Director of one of the country's largest NGOs. It was a challenging appointment which brought me into direct contact with large sections of physically challenged and underprivileged persons in the community. It was a very different view of the human experience for which I shall always remain grateful. I have already voiced my scepticism of armchair communists. One of the claims made by the extreme Left Wing of the Communist Party which held sway in West Bengal was the redistribution of land to landless farmers. At the village level, this translated into redistribution of non arable land to the landless! Landowning families who had leased out their properties to intermediate agents (jotedars) for fixed returns, never to return, continued to be wooed by the Left front in return for votes. When a section of the peasantry revolted against this unfair ownership and system of revenue collection, they were brutalised and rendered homeless. In a Government run primary school we visited there were no teachers or students. An eye witness confided that the children were asked to present themselves each morning with the sole purpose of signing an attendance register. They were dismissed immediately thereafter. The "teacher" was of course a party worker. I toured many villages in the Punjab, Gujerat, Maharashtra and Tamil Nadu only to discover that in matters like health care, literacy and womens' issues "a meal" as one celebrity writer put it, "is the only currency that is real." Casteism is still very prevalent in rural India. Whole communities belonging to the same village live apart from each other. They have their own wells, houses (more properly huts), even their own shrines for worship. Inter—caste dining or marriages are, of course, taboo.

To be born with any kind of handicap is possibly the worst curse in rural India. Families tend to regard a handicapped child as as someone who is paying for the sins of a previous birth. They are very often locked up or segregated from the other members of the family. The organisation I worked for had a scheme to reorient such persons and to train them in a particular trade or profession so that they could be brought into the mainstream. It was an initiative which succeeded where families lent their active support. In fact the transformation from negativism to attitudes of encouragement were palpable as soon as the handicapped person began contributing to the family income. Sheltered workshops and community training centres were some of the other options.

The experience of service to the community which Amita and I gained in Bombay inspired us to found Chetana Foundation for Social Awareness Research and Development (CFSARD). It was registered as a Public Charitable Trust in Mumbai, 1993. It is now 20 years old. Its main thrust was self help. We started out by training potential women entrepreneurs to help themselves and become financially independent. We took to promoting adult literacy because we felt there was a genuine need to create responsible citizens and more importantly responsible parents. We floated health care programmes in areas where the facilities were dismal and currently run two schools for non formal education of children in Dakshin Kashipur and Parasia in West Bengal upto Grade 5. CFSARD has also set up a Community Centre in Parasia. A committed team of members continue to promote awareness about Older persons in Mumbai. This particular issue which in India is fraught with increasing insecurity and deprivation among the elderly, particularly those who live in rural areas, was started by us in 1996 in recognition of the resolutions passed at the UN World Summit for Social Development at Copenhagen which recognised inter alia, a society for all ages—"one that adjusts its structures and functioning as well as its policies and plans, to the needs and capabilities of all, thereby releasing the potential for all for the benefit of all."

Needless to add, all these projects were initiated against the background of many social, economic and cultural inequities, not to mention the overall pathetic record of State intervention. There were other problems. No accurate statistical data was available in respect of any of these programmes. Political interference was rampant and the beneficiaries were either reluctant to accept new ideas or downright hostile in some cases. In the course of my travels across rural India I can recall at least one time when I wished I had Alladin's magic lamp strapped to my back. I also reminded myself that even poor old Alladin had to work to get his lamp going. He needed to rub it hard before the genie appeared. I have also reminded myself of the story of the man who blamed God because he never won a lottery until an exasperated God responded that he could only help provided the man would go out and buy that lottery ticket. The allusion is of course to the fact that nothing can be achieved until we are prepared to step out of our comfort zones.

Overall, it has been a great process of learning, motivation, marshalling new skills and working with groups of committed organisations like the National Association for the Blind and the Ramakrishna Mission. The Indian business sector and individual donors provided much needed resources but we felt there was need for a change in attitudinal responses. This is more easily said than done. One redeeming feature of Indian society is that it is by and large more amenable to community based rather than institutional welfare. In many areas it is also a gerontocracy. Therefore, one can probably safely assume that attempts at community based reform especially of the grass roots variety have a greater chance of succeeding where the provisions of the Indian Constitution and/or the Hindu Adoption and Maintenance Act has failed. Perhaps a day will come when the transition to a positive, active and developmentally oriented view of ageing and other societal problems may well result from action by older and younger people themselves, through the sheer force of their growing numbers and influence.

*   *   *

I have often been asked about my spiritual and religious inclinations. Although the women in our family, my grandmothers, my mother and my wife were all devout Hindus, I was never attracted to the outward trappings of my faith. Partly this was due to the fact that my father—at least ever since the time I knew him—was something of an agnostic, and partly because I was less than moved by the avariciousness and greed of our temple priests who seemed to make a living out of playing on people's superstitions and beliefs including some incredible practices described as being "auspicious" and inviolable. I realised later, that they knew next to nothing about the scriptures or of the symbolism behind Hindu iconic worship, much less about the philosophy of this great religion. The other thing that turned me off public worship were the crowds, the smells, the noise and the mud splattered watery floors which characterise most Hindu temples, particularly the more frequented ones. I have visited several across the length and breadth of this country. By and large this truism holds good. At a well known shrine near Bhubaneshwar we were threatened by the temple "panda" that something terrible would befall our newly born son if we refused to make a cash offering. On another occasion at another temple also in Bhubaneshwar and known throughout the world as one of the finest examples of Hindu architecture, I was pushed, shoved and hustled along with thousands of other devotees to touch the feet of the deity—actually to pour the contents of a container said to contain holy water, on the Shiv Linga—in a mad scramble of elbows, rotting flowers and sweat, to secure His blessings. The linga, is of course a symbolic representation of the male phallus and venerated by Hindus as an aniconic pillar of light to describe God, just as the Cross is symbolic of God in the abstract to devout Christians. South Indian temples are better organised and cleaner than most North Indian ones but even there, serious prejudices prevail. In Kanya Kumari, for example, I was refused entry into the temple because I was wearing trousers. The solution was equally startling. All I needed to do was to enter the sanctum with a dhoti wrapped round my trousers—a garment kept in reserve by the temple authorities and quickly loaned to tourists like myself, ignorant of the rules. In yet another shrine, worshippers were required to completely inundate themselves with holy water from several "kunds" to purify themselves before entering the sanctum.

My initiation into the Hindu faith began with a monk from the Ramakrishna Mission, Swami Nirlepananda (Kartick Maharaj), who became my spiritual guru at the tender age of 13. It ended, or should I say continues, with Vedanta, a philosophy as old as Sankara (8th Century AD) but which Swami Vivekananda revived—a philosophy drawn from the Upanishads which espouses individual and intuitional questing for truth as opposed to ritualistic social customs. Vedantists are committed to the diversity of all religions without compromising the teachings of the Vedas and the Upanishads and to find the common bases of Hinduism. Besides the fact that this approach appeals to reason and enlightened thought, I found that it also answered many of my own questions about spirituality and the faith into which I was born, for example, that all religions and religious philosophies are ultimately attempts at finding out the nature of the perceptible world—and of ourselves who perceive it ; that mythologies, deities, images and icons are merely symbols of the Immensity we call God or Divinity. We can look at a sculpture from different angles. We grasp its whole form only when we have observed the front, back and profiles. Each of these views is different from the others; some of the elements of their description may seem incompatible. Yet from these seemingly contradictory perceptions we can build up a general idea of the sculpture as a whole; that all Hindu gods and goddesses symbolise energies that represent aspects of the Divine power, best described as the SPACE-TIME-THOUGHT continuum. It is the absolute and ultimate stage in which are united—existence (the source of spatial form), consciousness or knowledge (the basis of thought) and limitless duration or eternity (the basis of experience or enjoyment).

These three elements, so say our philosophers, are held together by the Hindu triad BRAHMA (the creator and source of all rhythms, and all forms). VISHNU (the energy that creates cohesion and is also its protector) and SIVA or MAHESHWARA(who embodies the abysmal obscurity into which all activity in the end dissolves). Nothing that has existence can escape the process of destruction and it is from destruction that creation again arises. I suppose I am spiritual, not in the orthodox sense, necessarily, but in an intuitve way in which I see Immensity as the underlying oneness of all life, which makes so many human aspirations and striving seem rather unimportant. I believe that each one of us has a little bit of the Divine in him or her and that worship or meditation should consist in looking inwards, to develop one's consciousness about ourselves in relation to other living beings and our place in the universe. I think it is important to know how best we can serve others and also, that ultimately, each individual is reponsible to himself for his actions. My one regret is that I did not delve deep enough into the teachings of my guru to become a practising Vedantist. I confess I still look up to an external God especially in times of crisis! However the study of Hindu philosophy which includes among others, a knowledge of the deep symbolism behind our icons and popular forms of worship has made me more aware and tolerant of individual beliefs and observances. It has also helped me to understand, if not to actively participate in, the daily offerings made to our family deity.

Western writers and thinkers, barring a few notable exceptions have, throughout history, been slightly wary of the Hindus and their customs. In the early years of colonial rule eye witness accounts, especially of women like Elizabeth Fenton and Mary Sherwood describe a native community thriving on superstition and other acts of atrocity as terrifying reminders of a heathen

culture. Later Christ and Christianity came to symbolise
not just power but also Christian "benevolence." In
more modern times, a group of historians known as
the Orientalists postulated such concepts as the "eternal
and unchanging" character of the Hindu faith including
the misconception that everything in India is either
religious or spiritual. They dwelt on the fundamental
principles guiding practising Hindus viz. karma, dharma
and samsara without closely analysying the meaning
of these terms or of their relativity to a particular age
or community. In recent years, the Hindu Right by
espousing militancy in religious issues has caused even
more confusion by misinterpreting traditional sources.
One of the reasons for this confusion is undoubtedly
that Hinduism is not a doctrinaire religion like Judaism,
Christianity or Islam and that many of its central texts
cannot, as some scholars claim, be reliably dated even
within a century.

*   *   *

This account of my homecoming would be incomplete
without a mention of my older brother, Debkumar, who
impacted my life in more ways than one. The few years
he spent in this city during and after graduation, more
than five decades ago, saw a remarkable flowering of his
literary, artistic and intellectual accomplishments which
even today, contemporaries recall with admiration.
He was a poet, writer, painter and academic rolled
into one—a man of many parts, alas, who let his
extraordinary talents wither. This city, in particular,
remembers him as a founder member of the Writers'
Workshop, one of the first forums for Indian writing

in English, a great inter-collegiate debater, a dramatist and a painter with a distinctive style. In that brief period, he won many trophies and awards. Debkumar was my constant companion, playmate, bedfellow and in many ways my mentor, until well into adolescence. Many older brothers are jealous and bully their younger siblings into submission, but not this one. He was gentle, kind, always understanding and helpful—like Mother—and rarely raised his voice except under severe provocation. I was the big tease.

Growing up in Delhi, our major obsession was cricket. We both played badly but were great admirers of the game. Venues for practice sessions and friendly matches kept changing from one neighbouring house to another, our companions being children from these households, like the brothers Vinay and Ravindra Vyas or the Bhandarkars, Anand, Gopal and Viju. Sujit Bhattacharya and Arun Kanjilal are two other names that come to mind. Sometimes younger dependants of the domestic staff would join in. Excitement ran high when one or other of our friends would negotiate a friendly match with say the ruler of Alwar's "B" team or the Indian Air Force on their own manicured cricket grounds. On these occasions there were emergency recruitments to our motley group consisting of seasoned college going players, mainly fast bowlers and good batsmen. In the former category were Lahiri (I cannot remember his first name) and Anand Bhandarkar. Both swung the ball well. Lahiri was faster with a Ray Lindwall type delivery but erratic, compared to Bhandarkar who, eight times out of ten, bowled good length and had the opposition in trouble. Madhu, one of the Bhandarkars' dependants was a left arm spinner who also pitched and turned the ball well. Of the batsmen, Khokanda (Guha) was our idol. He usually went in at number three and wielded the willow with superb grace and style. In fact I can trace my own fascination with English cricket bats, a rare commodity in those days, from Khokanda's favourite short handled "Jack Hobbs". My brother and I were usually the last pair in and were invariably bowled or caught out in the first over. Before that there were innumerable fielding lapses and dropped catches for which curiously the rest of the team bore us no grudge. All this did not deter Debkumar from reading all the latest books on the game, memorising the MCC rules and preparing elaborate score cards. Because of this he was summoned on occasion to act as Umpire. I was more into pads, gloves and other accessories of the game.

We both learnt to swim at the nearby Gymkhana Club (The Imperial Delhi Gymkhana in those days). Our coach was a senior college student with a fine style. He taught me the freestyle the breast stroke and a modified version of the back stroke. My brother, always shy and self conscious, preferred to stick to the breast stroke to the exclusion of everything else. Sunday mornings were a special treat for us youngsters because we were permitted by our parents to sign for plates of potato chips accompanied by unlimited quantities of tomato sauce. Debkumar, an avid reader would wander off to the Club library where many boys and girls of his age also congregated. He was always looking for new ideas and one of his projects at this time was to produce a school tabloid which he edited. "The Columban" as it came to be called carried news of school events, student activities and contributions by his fellows. Coca Cola had just been launched in New Delhi at 4 annas (the equivalent of 0.25p) per bottle and "ice cold coke" as the billboards screamed, was the other obvious attraction. This was also the time when I learnt to ride a bicycle and to take my first driving lessons. Both skills proved to be of immense value then and in later life.

On occasion, we would wander off to the nearby "ridge" behind the house where we lived. This was an expanse of semi arid hillocks and undulating waste land surrounding central New Delhi with only a scattering of thorny "babla" trees for vegetation. It stretched all the way from Old Delhi and fascinated us by maps drawn up by the Survey of India identifying abandoned shrines and bridle paths. My brother, armed with an air rifle was always in charge of these expeditions He led me and some of our friends who were interested in joining, into what he loved to describe as "uncharted enemy territory" spotting and making notes of suspicious enemy movements, usually jackals, wild rabbits and squirrels, and other wildlife! Sometimes "enemy reconnaisance planes" would fly low over our heads and we were commanded to take shelter behind rocks and other bushes to avoid detection They were trainer aircraft from the nearby flying club!

There was no TV. All India Radio belted out news, music and talks with monotonous regularity so we were encouraged to develop extra curricular interests like learning to play the violin, Western style. Our tutor, an elderly Goan gentleman by the name of Noel Burton

Jones was very conscientous about his responsibilities. A bachelor, he lived alone and cycled to meet his students every week. We had a small chamber music group which included Laila Kabir, daughter of Independent India's first Minister of Education, Humayun Kabir and the three sons of the celebrity writer, Nirad C. Chaudhuri, one of whom (Kirti or Dhruba I cannot recall which) played the piano and the other, the viola. The third, Prithvi, was a couple of years younger than I. He too played the violin with remarkable skill for a boy of his age. Many years later I met up with Prithvi at the Tollygunge Club. Like me, he was by now old and had travelled round the world. He had developed a keen interest in photography and was taking pictures of the variety of wild life that even today inhabit the holy purlieus of that club, when I happened to spot him.

The other major attraction as children was travel. Over school holidays we made memorable road trips in the family car to exotic locations like Mandi, Kulu, the Kangra valley and Manali. At many of these places there were no tourist facilities except Government Inspection Bungalows and/or Circuit Houses for senior officers. The whole of Manali, for example, which we revisited many years later consisted of deodar forests apple orchards and an old temple of Hidimba Devi, where, legend has it, human sacrifices were the norm. The largest of the apple orchards was owned by a retired officer of the British Army, Major Banon, who married a local woman. The Banons built their house entirely of pinewood, and converted a part of it into a guest house for visitors. Today Manali is a tourist spot with an air strip. Nicholas Roerich, the Russian painter who married Devika Rani lived and painted in Kulu and the place was also famous for its fairs and beautiful people. Both Kulu and Manali are situated on the banks of the Beas which cascades down from the snows beyond in a raging torrent of emerald green and white foam. During longer breaks we would get away from the Delhi heat to escape to better known retreats like Simla or Dalhousie. Both were relatively unspoilt and still bore the unmistakeable stamp of the Raj. I recall one occasion when we stayed in a cottage of the Grand Hotel in Simla, with my father's personal orderly Lachman Singh as our security guard. One vacation was spent in a three bedroomed private villa in Dalhousie with "Patch" our pet cocker spaniel and Pratul Chowdhury (Minada) for company. Later after moving back to Calcutta, we spent similar vacations at Darjeeling, Mungpoo and Munsong. The two last named locations were cinchona plantations on the way to Kalimpong. They were accessed by a step winding mountain road at the time but once there, the environment was totally idyllic. There were no bazars or crowds, just the silence of the whispering pines and unrestricted snow views. Mungpoo was in additon associated with the memory of Rabindranath Tagore. The poet came to Mungpoo in 1938 and again in1939 at the invitation of Maitreyi Devi wife of Dr. M.M. Sen who was then the Quinologist. He lived and wrote in the very bungalow where we stayed as guests and where the locals are supposed to have celebrated his birthday before he died in1941. Today it is a museum.

I parted company with my brother shortly after he returned from Cambridge. I was then preparing to go abroad myself and we had a few months together. When

I returned to India after completing my studies, he had already left for the US with his girlfriend and fiancee to prepare for a Ph.d. at the University of Washington in Seattle. We saw each other rarely after that. Our first reunion took place almost 13 years later. In between, my parents would meet up with him when one or both of them travelled to the US on work. He had broken off his engagement and was in relationships with several other women from time to time. Nor did he complete his Post graduate work. He had secured a steady job and was always glad to see us whether at home or in America. Later he married an American girl and they had a son. Debkumar's reputation as a writer and an artist followed him to Cambridge University after which it all seemed to decline and fall by the wayside. He had already renounced his interest in the Jubilee Park house and turned his back on our parents when they died. The last time we met was in his new apartment in Bremerton, a small town across the Puget Sound from Seattle. He moved there after his wife died and was living the life of a recluse with his books and his collection of vintage wines music and DVDs.

*   *   *

I was never an avid reader at school and college. Writing came to me very late in life. It was something of a coincidence. After a visit to Vishnupur, the place where I was born, I felt I needed to communicate anecdotes and stories from my childhood and growing years to my immediate family, my children, their wives and our grandchildren who by this time were living away from us but have kept in touch with their roots. Very soon,

I stumbled upon the many potentialities of the pen (now a word processor!)—the freedom from routine, no targets or time frames and its incalulable resources. In many ways it was also a welcome escape from the Corporate world of idle gossip, jealousy, mistrust and vindictiveness. The other reason was that I needed an identity of my own, distinct from being known either as a corporate honcho or the son of a famous father. However, it soon became apparent that to become a successful author one would need to write something worth publishing, find honest people to publish it and identify sensible people to read it! Initially, I was diffident about confronting any of these issues. I never tried my hand at writing a novel but soon found that sincerity and convictions were part of my style. I recommend it to anyone who wishes to be a writer.

There are several other lessons I have learnt from life. First, that for most "insurmountable" problems the solution is usually at the end of one's own right arm. Second, there is a very real need to listen to (not just hear) what other people are saying. This implies empathy and understanding. In Management we learnt to respect the axiom "There are no bad workmen; only bad managers." Third, the good thing about bad times is that they don't last forever. "Without pain", said actress Angelina Jolie once, "there would be no suffering, without suffering we would never learn from our mistakes. To make it right, pain and suffering is the key to all windows, without it there is no way of life." Fourth that success and wish fulfilment come not only from hard work but from a generous measure of luck. You have to be at the right place at the right time and your face must fit. At all times, one needs to work without expecting any kind of reward. Fifth if people aren't ashamed of their own lifestyles, it pays to keep your mouth shut when in their company. The trouble with most of us is that we underestimate the power of simplicity. We tend to over complicate our lives by focussing on activities instead of results, and as the pace of life continues to race along in the outside world, we forget that we have the power to control our lives regardless of what is going on outside. Finally, no one, unless he or she is a hypocrite or liar, can hope to get away by claiming that they have never committed a mistake. The essential thing is to learn from your mistakes and to build on them. It is also true that many of life's tragedies are self created and that what constitutes disaster for you may be less than superficial for another.

In retrospect, no one can take your experiences away from you, however hurtful life's other encounters may be. The joys of a Delhi winter, watching cricket on the Feroze Shah Kotla ground from the President's box, the pageantry of Republic Day 1950, the Inauguration of the First Asian Games,1951, the beautiful garden houses in which we grew up, romping all over the Viceregal estate, swimming in the Viceroys' private pool, private audiences with Yehudi Menuhin and Ustad Vilayat Khan are only some of the memories which touch the peripheries of my childhood. There were many others.

*   *   *

I believe we have to keep reminding ourselves of the positives that create self confidence and build the kind of reserves to help dig up in your leaner years, the treasures you, and only you, possess. This does not necessarily include the creation of wealth, although in this day and age it is idle to pretend that material well being is unimportant. Indeed, academic achievements or the creation of wealth are just as worthy of merit as those of the creative artist, the musician and the artisan. It is a question of priorities. Happiness or the road to it, comes I think, by living in conformity with one's nature and one's capabilities and realising that character is moulded less by physical possessions or attributes than by one's environment and upbringing. It is also linked with a state of mind which can pick out those qualities which make each one of us unique, including basics like good health, good fortune, an uncomplicated family life and the opportunities that have helped us to understand ourselves, learn from our mistakes and relate with more sensitivity to people.

My own life experiences have been a mixture of the good and the bad. Although I confess I had the good fortune to be born into privilege and therefore had access to people and places not normally available to the average Indian citizen, I had to fight for virtually everything I wanted. Nothing, not even the perquisites of my job, came automatically, as they did for many others. I fought tooth and nail for the woman I wanted to marry because she belonged to a different caste and was a year senior to me in College. I lost my battle to read medicine because my father said he could not support me for five or six years through an MBBS degree and an internship. I could have done better for my second degree at London University if it did not clash with less than committed attempts at the Indian Administrative Service Examination. At work I struggled for my legitimate entitlements, including, at a very senior level, the flat occupied by my predecessor, a British national, in Bombay and membership of Clubs open only to foreigners at the time. Even as I rose to the second most senior position in my company, I was denied the legitimate grade and some of the perquisites that went with the job and on premature retirement from service, I was refused a pension, from the very fund I had helped to set up! It was difficult to accept at the time but I had to come to terms with the fact that I couldn't change the past, so I taught myself to look forward. I remembered reading somewhere that life was like a rope, twined in all its complexities and yet woven into one marvellous stream and that therefore, everyone has the chance to use something amazing from it. I did and have never looked back since. In any event, even if the end of my corporate career was somewhat grotesque, and ended so badly for all of us, I certainly do not regret the beginning or indeed, all of the intervening or subsequent years which gave us so much joy and many ecstatic moments of sheer delight.

Like most people, I had opportunities in life, some of which I took and others I let drop by the wayside. One of the reasons was that I was either unadventurous or just lazy when the opportunity occurred. A colleague would half jokingly say that I made the mistake, when the opportunity presented itself, of not "grabbing it and asking for more." In a manner of speaking he was right.

Grabbing an opportunity could lead to many others. The principle applies equally in social and professional life. A certain amount of curiosity and drive are also necessary to make things happen. "No risk, no gain" is a favourite saying among people who regard success as a matter of making choices. Nothing ever happens by wishful thinking alone. You have to get your foot in the door. The worst that can happen is that you will be met with a refusal.

In the last twenty years or so I can think of many such opportunities that came my way which, had I not seized and followed up in time, would have left us all in relative despair. The first was a formal meeting in Bombay with the Director of the Secretariat for U.N. International Year of the Family in Vienna, in 1993. Chetana had just been registered as a Public Charitable Trust and we were desperately looking out for funding support. The U.N. does not normally support private projects. However, after six months of protracted correspondence, we were able to get not just a foothold but a grant from one of their constituent members. Chetana was featured in the official UN Project catalogue for that year, which in turn gave us the required credibility and leverage with many public and private sector banks in India. Not dissimilar was my encounter in 1994 with Dr Hans Schenk, a Dutch Professor of Economics who was staying in the same Guest house as I, in New Delhi. Neither of us knew the other but I thought I would introduce myself and we got talking. The meeting resulted in a personal recommendation from Dr Schenk to a Public Charitable Trust in the Netherlands which has continued its support to Chetana ever since. In

2009, a meeting with the then Managing Member of the Tollygunge Club led to an invitation to Amita and I to write the history of that Club. The book, a runaway success, was launched by the then Governor of West Bengal, Shri Gopal Krishna Gandhi. So was the creation of the Club Library, spearheaded by a Committee I chaired in the first fledgling years of its existence and considered by many to be a pioneering initiative in the Club's 118 year old history. In Bombay, 2010 while staying with a well known painter friend, I met another old acquaintance, who without any questions asked, was kind enough to give me an introduction to the Cama Institute of Oriental Studies. At the time I had begun work on the religious architecture of Colonial Calcutta but never for a moment imagined it would lead to an invitation to deliver their 180th Memorial Lecture on the same subject, six months later! Likewise meetings in Bombay in 2010 with MARG, India's leading Art Journal led to an article being published one year later, in their October 2011 issue. Nobody in our family had ever written for MARG before. It was a journal we admired from a distance for its high quality of writing and photographs. If this was not enough I was invited by the Birlas to spearhead a project to produce a Family Charities Album on terms I ended up dictating. They were more favourable than my entire Provident Fund and Gratuity put together! Finally, the story of Bloomsbury was a remarkable coincidence, an unexpected gift. Years of fruitless search for a publisher ended suddenly one afternoon when a representative from Macmillan visiting Calcutta found out about the work I was doing. He said he was interested and persuaded me to risk leaving a copy of the manuscript with him. It was a decision fraught with uncertainty because the particular division of Macmillan closed down shortly afterwards. Six months and several sleepless nights later, I was relieved to learn he had joined Bloomsbury as Senior Consulting Editor and that the book would be published by them as part of their first instalment of non fiction writing by Indian authors in this country. Being bracketed with a publishing giant like Bloomsbury on my first ever solo venture as a writer was beyond my wildest dreams but I had succeeded in establishing an identity of sorts. More than euphoria, I felt totally vindicated and fulfilled.

On the flip side of the coin, there were many missed opportunities, like the time I was undecided whether to invest in real estate in Chennai, where, even in the 1970s, property was being bought and sold at throwaway prices. Around the same time we were offered a 900 sqft flat on Malabar Hill with a small garden and a sweeping view of Queens Necklace for Rs 2,00,000 which I declined in favour of Company accommodation in Hill Park. That flat would today fetch anything between Rs 40-50 crores. Likewise, in 1984, I sold off some 200 Blue Chip Shares on an impulse. Today they would be worth a small fortune. I did not take full advantage of the teachings of my spiritual guru and given the wonderful opportunities which came my way, I might have paid more serious attention to my music. These and many other decisions I took or did not take at the time could have resulted in changing the whole course of my life, for better or for worse I do not know.

The point is that people's priorities differ and although every human will has the power to transform its fate, you have to be responsible to yourself and to your conscience. To quote Shantaram, the hero of a novel of that name, "No matter what kind of game you find yourself in, no matter how good or how bad the luck, you can change your life with a single thought" Other people may think differently but I have no regrets for any of my actions. Consider what might have happened if my AVR surgery in 2007 had gone awry! Or if in the depths of some of our most difficult periods of stress, one or both of us were to be permanently disabled or incapacitated. I always dreamt of the good life and at varying periods fancied a career abroad. At the same time I was conscious that I could never jump out of my skin, much less settle abroad permanently. Over the years people and circumstances have changed and the global village has shrunk to far more manageable levels. Today we are all international citizens but you still have to be lucky enough to belong somewhere, and that belonging is tied to your roots. In Calcutta or Kolkata, whatever you choose to call this city, I can crave the indulgence of old associations, memories and places. I meet up with Kajori, a face which had disappeared from memory fifty years or more ago and reappeared in the warmth of an embrace with the words that this should have happened when we were both young and unmarried! I meet a gentle person like Pranab Ghosh who works for the Gun and Shell Factory in Cossipore but writes the most sensitive and thought provoking verse, and I pass a bus stop which reminds me that this is where I first took the initiative to accost the woman who is now my wife. Where else in metropolitan India would one expect to wake to the chirping of birds or to the mournful call of the hawker who makes a living out of selling "phooljharus" or to experience at first hand the skill and the syncopated rhythms of the "dhakis" at Durga Puja? Like Gopal Krishna Gandhi's India, Calcutta is like a mirror shattered into a thousand relecting fragments. You have to relate to one or other of these fragments. In the process of integration, it is the projection of the values you have imbibed that make for character, not in their denial. Life is much too short and precious for such frivolities—a thought I would be happy to share with any like minded person of my generation and/or members of the next.

I look at the clock and see the seconds ticking by. Time seems to be rushing past, and the days and nights, all too short for comfort. So, if it is not too late to bless the lucky stars in my life for all the incredible memories I was fortunate to have shared with the family into which I was born—and later tried to recreate—with my own, I would like to do so now. As one grows older, one has to be grateful even for small mercies like a pair of intact hands and feet, two eyes, a healthy physique and a life free of physical and mental worries or handicaps. It would be nice to make my final exit also, in this way, without much fuss and without making a nuisance of myself to others. Very soon, to quote another Bob Hope quip, even the birthday suit will need pressing! I really have no desire to be reborn although our 'shastras' claim that one is bound to be reborn as long as there is an iota of desire left, even subconsciously, in the mind.

Memories are a form of desire—an indulgence which waves to you from a distance and is gone; but the good ones are also the stuff of life. It is reassuring to know you can pick them up and arrange them in your mind's eye when needed. I have always nursed a strong desire to surround myself with beauty and have been genuinely interested in people, especially creative people. Perhaps in my next birth, if there is a next birth, I will be born as one, more appropriately, as a celebrity with plenty of money. The negative side is that I may not be half as lucky. Creative people always seem to have so much at stake and face countless hardships and disappointments. To think of only a few, great painters or musicians, even the great bard of Bengal, Rabindranath Tagore, have all gone through the most turbulent and harrowing experiences in their emotional lives. Gaugin painted in exile in Tahiti, Vincent Van Gogh cut off his ear in a moment of acute frustration, Henri de Toulouse Lautrec was a cripple, Rembrandt spent the last few days of his life in penury, and Mozart struggled throughout his life for money besides domestic upheavals with his father and wife. Nearer home, the Sufi mystic Lalan Fakir was stoned for his unorthodox views on religion and man/woman relationships, and the great Ustad Bade Ghulam Ali Khan was too poor to be able to pay for his treatment when he died. The list is endless. I would therefore like to indulge in some wishful thinking and say once again that I would like if possible to be born to the same set of parents, and to have the same wife, children, grandchildren and friends with whom I have been blessed, in this life. If this sounds like a lot of garbage, rest assured that I am speaking figuratively—of the souls which inhabit or have inhabited these bodies in the past—souls which are eternal and unchanging, and not necessarily related to their physical likenesses. Like my father before me, I may not be able to leave much in the way of material possessions for my family. As long as they continue to respect the virtues of truth, tolerance, kindness and contentment—which, I believe, constitute the basics of the human story—they will not be sorry.

An intrinsic part of my mental makeup has been to question established custom or conventional wisdom. The style did not appeal to everyone because it led to controversies. Today, I find I can make plenty of allowances for people's opinions, beliefs and even dogmas, although I am still allergic to liars, mental and physical lethargy and rudeness. I lead an active life. I walk, I swim, I drive, ride a bike and am reasonably computer savvy. I love to travel, enjoy a lively party, read, write and listen to good music. Overall it has been a charmed life. From the climb to Lamadug near Manali—crossing the snowline and several fast flowing mountain streams with a wife and two children barely 10 and 6 on an expedition which could have ended in disaster; or my posting to Madras (Chennai), which miraculously took us away from the culture of violence and massive power outages which overtook the state in the late 60's and 70's; or finding profitable and creative avenues for my skills after retirement—fortune, in all its glory, has been kind. Indeed, it has been a humbling experience. Today I am on the other side of the table, an employer of sorts, and beyond manipulation by anyone. The wheel might well have turned the other way. I should like, therefore, to end with a quote from a favourite Shakespearean passage. Here it is:

"Sweet are the uses of adversity
Which, like the toad, ugly and venomous
Wears yet a precious jewel in his head
And this our life, exempt from public haunt
Finds tongues in trees, books in the running brooks
Sermons in stones and good in everything.
I would not change it."

*   *   *

CHAPTER 2

My Father

My father was a rebel if ever there was one. He rebelled against an autocratic and over protective parent by escaping from the stifling atmosphere of his home in Dhaka. He rebelled against society and social convention when he married Ma, then a mere teenager, from a different caste. He rebelled against corruption and nepotism in government and resigned from the ICS. The fact that he did all this with a clear conscience was ample proof of his determination to be self sufficient, which is why he never thought of himself as the conventional Bengali patriarch. Without doubt, the job he held provided certain securities and privileges denied to the average householder, such as admissions for his children to the best schools in the country, free medical treatment for himself and his family and a lifelong pension for his wife if she survived him. He respected individual liberty and freedom of thought—upto a point—and always upheld the principle of guidance by precept rather than by force or compulsion Matched only by the glittering trappings of his office, the palatial homes in which we lived and the eulogies of friends and relatives combined with his academic brilliance, gave him an aura of uncommon distinction which we came to respect and love.

In the decades in which we grew up, fathers were rarefied commodities. You saw them infrequently. When you did, it was to ask a favour such as pocket money or to write an "excuse" to your class teacher for absence or because you did not wish to take part in PE. You saw them of course, large as life, when it came to matters of discipline, including permissions and sanctions of every kind. Ours was more accessible and indulgent. As a toddler I was captivated by his eyes which shone with an uncanny brilliance, but more so by his glasses! A photograph from the family album of me, aged two, records this fascination for Baba's "champa" for posterity. How he could be so generous with something as precious as glasses (there was no acrylic in those days and visits to the ophthalmologist were expensive) I do not know, but it could be a game he liked to play. He was something of a tease. I recall chasing him round the house with a kitchen knife when I was four about something trite, and indeed at age six or seven we argued with him about how young girls hated to go out with old men! There were others. Another game we played was to jump into bed with Ma on winter mornings and letting him brave it out in the cold!

Being a younger son, I escaped most of Baba's attention and ire when it came to academics. Dada, my older brother, was the brain. By comparison, I was plain mediocre. Baba was very strict about study and mealtimes. For as long as I can remember, all weekends and holidays, barring a few notable exceptions were divided into (a) early morning study (6:30-8:00am) (b) late morning study (10:00-12:30pm (c) afternoon study (2:30pm-4:30pm) and (d) evening study (7-8:30pm). No amount of academic excellence, like the scholarship I won for standing first among 4th graders across all Christian Brothers' Schools in India made any impact on this schedule. That we did not turn into zombies was entirely due to Ma who encouraged other pursuits, music and painting and even sports like swimming, cycling and cricket as leisure activities. As we grew older I developed a passion for languages. French was an automatic choice. It was taught at school by a particularly colourful teacher who thought the world of my accent and general linguistic aptitudes. This suited Baba because at that point he was going to Geneva to attend an ILO Conference and I was his sounding board. I cannot remember how often we sat down to board games. Howeve I do recall he joined us to play "Draughts" and to a lesser extent "Ludo" and "Monopoly." "Meccano" and "Hornby" train sets were popular. So were toy cars which you drove round the house making a frightful racket, rocking horses and the mandatory tricycle. Baba was never particularly demonstrative about his affections but we knew he was in one of his indulgent moods when he would suddenly think of buying us the odd inexpensive gift—like chocolates, a pair of socks, even an undershirt.

As children we were captivated by some of Baba's "treasures", among others a Webley and Scott revolver, his array of gold medals, his LSE blazer, suits from Austin Reed, his box of solar topees and many souvenirs from America including a three dimensional View Finder and a beautiful white tuxedo which I hoped I would inherit one day! I learned to drive at the tender age of 15. Baba never once thwarted my efforts. Instead he accompanied me to the driving test and signed the papers confirming my eligibility. To this day my Driving Licence bears the imprint of his handwriting and signature.

One of Baba's disarming qualities was his lightheartedness and ability to laugh at himself—the times when he would unguardedly drop his regular Bengali accent for a word or phrase in the dialect of his native East Bengal or when soon after his return from England, he asked for his Hilsa to be boiled instead of having it cooked the way most Bengalis do, in mustard sauce. His other attributes were restraint, lack of any major vices and the ability to spend time with his books and his typewriter in favour of whiling away precious hours at a bar or a Club. However he was very devoted to his friends from college and regularly attended meetings of the Presidency College Alumni Association.

Baba was something of an agnostic. He renounced the rigidities and superstitionns of the Hindu faith but never interfered with anyone's religious beliefs or customs. He was an achiever and a pragmatist, highly organised and meticulous to the last detail. During their 60 years of marriage, he supported Ma in everything she did including a Bachelors Degree, her painting and pursuit of Indian Classical music. His relations with his own parents were formal but laced with a sense of duty and responsibility. He was more at home with his in-laws. However his introverted nature did not permit him to share his disappointments with others. I recall he wept on my shoulder at his father's funeral murmuring how he had failed "everybody."

The day Baba died is still clearly etched in my memory. He had developed a chest cold and was clearly having difficulty in breathing. I gave him his last dose of medicine, a cough syrup and went out to the neighbouring bank on an urgent errand. By the time I returned, he was gone. He lay there, just as I had left him, looking peaceful and happy. The trauma of the moment was framed in memories—some quite insignificant ones—like he time he taught me how to unpack a new shirt or the security of the hand that held mine during my first ever sea bath in the turbulent waters of the Bay of Bengal. One of these was the story of the time he rubbed his cheek on my baby feet, lovingly promising to be my slave for life. That meant so much to me at the time, because he was usually so reticent.

CHAPTER 3

Beltala Beat

As children, Sukumar Ray's allegoric "Nara" (pronounced "Narah" as in "Sarah" to describe a hairless or shaven headed individual) was a source of constant delight and amusement. The anecdote about a king seated on a pile of bricks munching peanuts which he "ate but did not swallow", with nothing better to do than to seriously contemplate how many times "Nara" was likely to walk under a Bel tree for fear of being struck by its falling fruit, was as completely insane as was its inherent satire. The satire was about a ruler's preoccupation with inconsequentials and, figuratively, his inability to swallow what he ate. Sukumar Ray was of course Bengal's very own Edward Lear and this particular poem was among his first in the collection known as "Abol Tabol."

The city of Kolkata abounds in romantic place names such as Badamtala, Nimtala, Beltala, Kadamtala, Keoratala and many others. However, none of these have links to their origins or character—least of all Beltala, meaning a grove of Bel trees. Indeed, any resemblance to Sukumar Ray's concept of such a grove must be purely coincidental, except perhaps his symbolic description of an anarchic, peanut munching king wearing an oversized crown. Today, Beltala, the Headquarters of Bengal's Public Vehicles Department, is a maze of ugly, ill planned high rise apartments surrounding a modest red brick building dating back to the Raj. The place echoes to the bustle of motor cars, autos, taxis and commercial vehicles belching smoke to remind one of Kolkata's gentler past and its evolving diabolic contrasts. More importantly, Beltala is a symbol of the apathy and misgovernment that residents and visitors alike have come to associate with this city. When one considers that there are over 500 touts active in the Beltala office, most of them belonging to the CPM affiliated Trade Union, CITU, and that an estimated 15000 people visit Beltala every day for vehicle registrations, licences, fitness certificates and similar chores, the magnitude of their operations is immediately evident. The touts have been permitted by the party in power to function on the premises on the plea that they are there to save people from "harassment by Government officials." They end up charging 2 or 3 times the regular fees for their services. Needless to add the police are mute spectators to the drama.

Resident vehicle owners, need to visit Beltala several times in their lifetimes. Fortunately, because of postings outside the State, I was spared the trouble. Besides, all routine documentation in connection with running a motor car were taken care of by the local authorities in those cities. After retirement we returned home and for the first time began to experience some of the trials and tribulations which compel visitors to Kolkata to either forget or ignore their immediate surroundings. Last July, six months before my Driving Licence was due to expire, I sent out feelers about its renewal to the authorities here. Their response was not encouraging. Nobody in the present set up was able to identify an India Driving Licence, the kind issued to owner drivers in the fifties and sixties, with several folds and flaps illustrating basic road rules. The fact that there was no photograph was an added disincentive. At the top of the document was a space to enter one's name and address including changes of residence if any. Mine showed that I had moved house twice, once from Calcutta to Madras (Chennai) and then from Madras to Bombay (Mumbai). However because the licence was last renewed in Mumbai, and technically still valid, there was no mention of our current home address. Had I registered my change of address? Was I aware that West Bengal was now no longer in the Middle Ages and that I needed a Smart Card? The answer to both questions was of course in the negative. That settled it. There was no question of revalidation. Although it was issued in Calcutta, the old licence would need to be scrapped. The only way out was to apply for a fresh Driving Licence, complete with driving test. I saw little point in arguing that Mumbai had renewed my old licence without a fuss and that driving licences were freely sold, under the protective arm of CITU, right here, in the holy purlieus of Beltala, to people who could not drive. My own experience of driving not only in India but across the UK and the US was, as I hated to point out to the man at the counter, probably more than his years. However, to expect a change of heart or intent appeared futile.

Recapitulating the warmth of forgotten summers, I went back in time to that morning when as a young adolescent, fresh out of school, I accompanied my father to the same Department for my first ever driving test. I remembered the meticulous care with which I studied traffic and road signs, and recalled being reminded how my newly acquired skills would place additional responsibilities on my young shoulders as a considerate driver and citizen of this country. I remembered the uncluttered spaces and a uniformed Inspector in the adjoining seat, putting me politely but firmly through my paces. His concluding appraisal of my driving abilities was to ask if I could reverse into a designated parking space. Right now, I was staring at a piece of incomprehensible legislation framed by persons who had deliberately turned their backs on the law.

Abject surrender is usually not an option in these circumstances. The inevitable followed and I was soon among a group of dubious looking Dickensian characters—the kind anyone would avoid accosting on a dark street at night. Papers were strewn all over a table in a dingy office on top of a garage overlooking the main courtyard. The person in charge accepted my initial offer of Rs 500 without a murmur or a receipt. I was of course reminded that he was owed another Rs 1000 after the completion of all formalities. The application was for a Learner's Licence in the first instance and I would be summoned for a driving test a month and a half later. He hoped I had at some point sat behind the wheel of a motor car but not to worry if I hadn't. His people would be present to "help out" if needed. Six weeks later, I was queuing up with my driver and at least 50 other hopefuls at the testing ground. They were all accompanied by relatives or batmen whose main responsibilities were to locate their respective touts/agents for a smooth passage through the "test." We paid Rs 20 to hire a couple of "L" plates. These were hurriedly attached by means of wires to the front and rear fenders of the car to proclaim that all of us were indeed "learners." Our tout waved a tattered piece of paper under my nose, containing prints of road and traffic signs with English and Bengali sub titles. He pleaded with me to memorise them should the Inspector question my understanding of the symbols. The actual "test" was equally absurd. The Inspector looking more like a Kafkaesque figure behind dark glasses than a paid Government official, poked his head through the window to check if the name and photograph on the application form tallied with mine. Thereafter, he stood back and asked that I drive round the block accompanied only by my driver. A young girl barely into her twenties in the car before me was asked merely to pull her vehicle out of the parking lot to earn her credentials. My own driving test was over but there were other formalities. I would need to return to the office to get myself photographed by a computer and leave thumb impressions for the actual Smart Card. This would of course take another three weeks. So what was the actual fee for a new licence, I asked a Departmental employee on the way out. Four hundred and fifty rupees, came the laconic reply.

Beltala has an unenviable reputation. Legal procedures are seldom followed and a report in the press once quoted the CITU Secretary as saying that "These people (the touts) are making a living in an unorganized way, so we have decided to grant them affiliation." Another press report examines the data available with Bhagwandas Vehicle Testing Services, which runs the designated meter-testing facility at Salt Lake stadium. According to this agency, almost 14,000 taxis plying in the city have ignored the transport department's notification issued eight months ago to get their meters calibrated. The Secretary of the Association is reported to have claimed that out of 17284 taxis that came to the centre to have their meters calibrated almost 40 per cent showed readings higher than the actual chargeable fare for a particular distance. The registration numbers of the taxis that did not turn up to get their meters tested are available with both the transport department and Bhagwandas Vehicle Testing Services but no action has been initiated against them. The notification issued by the transport department had made it mandatory for all taxis registered with the public vehicles department's office in Beltala and the regional transport offices in Alipore, Barasat, Howrah and Barrackpore to get their meters calibrated at the Salt Lake centre every six months or face a fine of up to Rs 3,000.

Not a single taxi has, however, been booked in the past eight months for not getting its meter calibrated. A senior PVD official said the department was unable to continue the crackdown because it was "severely understaffed".

Kolkata's pollution levels, due mainly to automobile emissions, are sufficiently well known not to require elaboration. The menace of "kata tel", a mixture of bootlegged aviation fuel naptha and petrol continue to plague the people of this city because of the nexus between politicians and corrupt vehicle operators, while superannuated vehicles ply the roads without a care in the world because they are protected by the ruling party. Clearly an overhaul of the Public Vehicles Department is long overdue. If Sukumar Ray's "Nara" was his king's only preoccupation, the author's prophetic vision of our rulers sitting on their high horses, oblivious to the circumstances surrounding them, surely matched his bizarre and somewhat chaotic sense of humour.

CHAPTER 4

An Odyssey Of Sorts

The labyrinthian alleyways of Hyderabad's Lad Bazar are comparable in some ways to the 'gullies' of Varanasi and, figuratively, to the mazes of Hampton Court. They are not only a remarkable landmark but are part of a tradition that has survived over six centuries of the city's history. Lad Bazar extends to the west of the Charminar. This "monumental gateway" in the words of William Dalrymple "formed by a quadrant of arches rising to four domed minarets" is Hyderabad's very own symbol of its Nawabi origins. The area, known as Purana or Mitti ki Sheher is dominated by beautiful mosques, great arches or 'kamans' and chowks or squares which have managed to retain some of their medieval flavour despite the traffic congestion caused by bicycles, motor cycles, carts, three wheelers and pedestrians, all jostling for space in their bid to beat the ever present spectre of obsolescence and decay.

Lad Bazar is the quintessential Oriental market. It is said to have been founded by Ladi Begum, wife of Mir Mehboob Khan and Mehboob Chowk is where his concubines lived. Another story of its origins goes back to the Qutb Shahi dynasty when it was called the Lords' Bazar or the Bazar of the nobles. The street known as Moti ki Gully is one of India's finest and best wholesale markets for pearls. Other picturesque names, each denoting a specific craft, trade or occupation are known as Chudi Bazar, Joda Bazar, Judwa Bazar, Meena Bazar, and so on. In tiny upper story apartments accessed by rickety wooden stairs sit traders, craftsmen and tailors of every description. They range from collectors of beautiful artefacts belonging to former nawabs, old booksellers, metalware and woodcraft workers, embroidery and jewellery craftsmen and even birdsellers.

Many years ago I used to visit an old Pandit in Mitti ki Sheher who traded in antiques. He was a man in his mid fifties and his 'shop' was an improvised store room on the ground floor of the house in which he lived. You accessed the house after passing an imposing but crumbling stone arch straddling the road, turning right where the road ended, then left and finally left again. Panditji was well known in the neighbourhood and you only had to mention his name to command immediate attention. He was known to trade in a variety of antiques collected from old Nawabi homes. I was fascinated by the variety of crystal including exquisite lamps, chandeliers, wine glasses, decanters, mirrors of all shapes and sizes, oil paintings, bronzes and marbles, which were all well beyond my reach. Bargaining was difficult because Panditji would size up his customers very quickly and sooner than expected, would separate the wheat from the chaff. I was forewarned not to display my ignorance and usually ended up carrying away small pieces of crystal capable of being transported as personal baggage on an aircraft and thereafter, reassembling the pieces at home. Among my favourites were a pair of single candle stands with delicately matching etched crystal glass shades. They adorned our dining table for many years until we moved house. Then the stands gave way and we were left with the two crystal shades.

Lad Bazar and Mitti ki Sheher hadn't changed in thirty years. The old clock tower, the green and white Chowk Mosque with its various workshops and vendors, the Hotel Mohammadi with its smell of hot spiced kababs mingling with the aroma of tea, down to the shops where I once lingered longingly to pick up a pair of pearl pendants and the occasional Gadhwal sari, were all still there. So was the traditional Hyderabadi hospitality as we were soon to discover.

Cars and other heavy vehicular traffic are not permitted beyond the Charminar. So we left ours at a convenient parking lot and proceeded on foot—the mission, to rediscover my Panditji. Although the surroundings were familiar, we had obviously taken a wrong turn. My landmark, the old archway was missing. For one horrible moment I thought it might have been razed to the ground. A friendly shopkeeper reassured me it had not and suggested a diversion which unfortunately led to numerous other alleyways all headed in different directions. Things were beginning to look a little desperate. Then somebody pointed to a carved door. He guessed this might be the address we were looking for. I was certain he was wrong

An old lady was watching TV as we entered and introduced ourselves. Beyond the room in which she sat was a covered courtyard displaying an old chandelier several mosque lamps and old Tanjore paintings. Surrounding her were more Tanjore paintings porcelain figures, old clocks and bronzes. Although she was surrounded by this wealth of antiquity she appeared totally disinterested in us or our mission. Presently, a younger woman appeared. She recognized my Panditji instantly and explained that the house in which we were seated belonged to his nephew, her husband. The old Pandit had, of course, died and the family had given up selling antiques. They were now into the more lucrative business of gold and silver jewellery. She too reassured me the old archway was still standing and that her husband, who, by this time had been informed of our visit, was on his way back to meet us. This unexpected pleasure was accompanied by cups of steaming hot tea.

Panditji's nephew, Jaikaran, was a man in his mid fifties. Behind a genial countenance which reminded me of his late uncle he appeared to wield some influence in the neighbourhood. He brought out photographs of two of his uncles and wondered if I could identify the one I knew. His curiosity satisfied, he proceeded to ask how he could help. Jaikaran had arrived on his motorcycle but said the landmark I had missed was within walking distance! We left the house and sauntered past two well fed cows lazing in the sun munching grass. There, not

20 yards from where we stood, on a street parallel to the one which led us to Jaikaran's house, was my lost archway! It stood in all its fading glory—a fine piece of Indo Saracenic architecture which had doubtless seen better times. It was easy enough to imagine how, in days gone by, it had resounded to the sights and sounds of the numerous vendors displaying their wares and how merchants and traders from across the world in their flowing robes had passed under its portals.

I explained to Jaikaran the purpose of our visit which was to secure if possible, an exact replica of one of the crystal lampshades I picked up from his uncle's collection over three decades ago. It was one of those tragic cases of carelessness. A few days before we left home, someone not used to coping with antique glass had thoughtlessly dropped and broken one. I had no idea if it could be replaced, much less of its actual value or measurements. Jaikaran looked thoughtful at first and then suggested I hop on to the rear seat of his motorbike. Then followed a seemingly endless ride through the narrow alleyways of Mitti ki Sheher with one of my hands clinging on to the guard rail behind and the other clutching my travel wallet. I had not been on a motorcycle for a good forty years and neither Jaikaran nor I were wearing helmets. However, like a true Hyderabadi, my host thought it best not to bother with such trivialities, so I decided I would sit back and enjoy the experience.

We finally emerged into a torpid looking square—Jaikaran called it the Murga Bazar—which by its name, I guessed, was old Hyderabad's wholesale market for chicken. It was lined with several shops selling antiques some of which had not yet opened even though the time on my watch showed 11:45 in the morning. A few minutes later Jaikaran had dived into another alley past an old automobile workshop into an open courtyard. We were greeted by a comely old bearded gentleman who seemed to have been expecting us. We dismounted and without further ado, followed him to a padlocked room upstairs. There on the floor were lined at least a hundred lampshades of all shapes and sizes of the type I had come to look for! Among all the distractingly different pieces I finally picked one that looked like a close match and promptly closed the deal. It could only be packed with old newspapers to serve as dunnage, but the problem was how to carry it back on Jaikaran's motorbike.

On the ride back, I clung to my newly acquired treasure like a log on a rolling sea, ignoring the guard rail and parking the travel wallet securely between my knees. Sensing my discomfort Jaikaran drove back slowly to a point not far from his house where cars were permitted. He had already contacted the driver on his mobile 'phone and the car was waiting. His wife meanwhile had kept company with mine plying her with more tea and chatting her up with stories of the family and their social customs.

Jaikaran's parting gesture was to hand me a note to a friend in an Emporium where I could pick up a Gadhwal sari at a ten percent discount if I wished. Bidding goodbye to this extraordinarily hospitable couple was also a kind of farewell to Mitti Ki Sheher and my Panditji. It had been an encounter full of patient understanding and uncommon ingenuity, and for us, a journey into the past, an opportunity to sample, at first hand, the disappearing tranquility and gentility of old Hyderabad. It was also more than rewarding to discover on our return to Calcutta that my new find matched the old in all its beauty, down to the last etched leaf.

CHAPTER 5

Land Of The Lost Gods

The tragedy of the devastation caused by the Khmer Rouge in Cambodia has been compounded by the looting and pillaging of ancient temples including the world famous complex of Angkor Wat. It has left in its wake a series of decapitated statues, mutilated monuments and above all, the loss of incalculable information about the past. Angkor Wat and its surrounding temples have now been taken over by the UNESCO. The architectural park in which these timeless monuments are situated has been declared a World Heritage site. However, across the Cambodian countryside, the vandalising of other equally ancient historical sites continues. According to APSARA, the official Cambodian agency charged with the management of the Angkor Archaeological landscape, the local populace is involved, supported by powerful intermediate foreign agencies.

President Pratibha Patil's expressions of wonder and amazement at the beauty of Angkor Wat at the time of her recent visit, merely accentuate the enthusiasm of millions of tourists who visit Seam Reap each year. The culture and religion of Cambodia and its people, the Khmers, is of course Buddhist. However the early influence of Hindu traditions, iconography and beliefs in these temples is unmistakable. It is the impeccable blend of these two streams that make fusion convincing. Secondly, Cambodia's temples—specifically Angkor—date back to the 9th and 11th centuries if not earlier. This gives them an antiquarian and therefore archaeological interest. Maurice Glaize, a mid 20th century conservator of Angkor compared the architecture of these temples to the architecture of ancient Greece and Rome. The first efforts at conservation began in 1908 and continued throughout the last century except for a period of about 20 years during the Vietnam War. Thirdly, like the pyramids of ancient Egypt, the casual visitor is awestruck by the manner in which these massive stone structures were built to conform to precise geometric configurations without recorded mechanical or technical support. From the dramatic view of Angkor Wat across the moat to nearby Angkor Thom, Ta Prohm, Bayon, the South Gate and the Banteay Srei Complex, the whole scenario is fascinating and challenging. Angkor is instantly memorable, besides working insiduously on the imagination.

The Khmer rulers who built these temples bear names suggesting distinctly Indian origins. Prominent among these are Yasovarman I (c889-c915), Rajendravarman (c944-c968), Suryavarman I (c1002-c1049), Suryavarman II (c1113-c1150), Jayavarman VII (c1181-c1220) and Jayavarman VIII (c1243-c1295). As is well known, Varma, Varman or Burman is a Kshatriya title commonly affixed to some ruling families of India. The word "Khmer," according to an old (948 AD inscription) derives from the union of Prince Svayambhuva Kambu from Arya Desa (India) and a commoner Mera. Unfortunately these assumptions lack proper authentication. Theories about possible genealogical links between the Khmer rulers and their ancestral counterparts in India are legion. One assumption is that Prince Nandivarman II who was in fact the love child of his father and a Cambodian princess was brought to India to take over the throne after the death of the Pallava King Parameswaravarman II of Kanchi (c728-c732), for want of a male heir. Another, more plausible hypothesis is that Cambodia or Kambodge as the French called it, derives its name from the Sanskrit Kamboja and that this was also the name of the Indo-Iranian tribe who migrated to India from Central Asia. One such group who settled in Gujerat and Saurashtra migrated to South East Asia, to establish not just cultural but political and historic links with this country. In fact, Prince Svayambhuva Kambu, referred to earlier, was the leader of that tribe. This also explains the adoption of North Indian city names like Ayodhya, Mathura, Kusumpura, Hastinapura, Dvaravati and others in this region. The Kambojas had of course set up alliances with the Sakas, Pallavas and Yavanas in South India which could explain the Pallava connection. This is corroborated by numerous legends about the origins of Kambuja's ruling family. Ancient Sanskrit texts like Kautilya's Arthasastra attest that besides being formidable warriors the Kambojas were merchants excelling in trade and agriculture. In the 1st Century AD, numerous Indians migrated to Java including Prince Guna Varman, grandson of the King of Kabul who visited China by way of Sri Lanka and Java. Guna Varman renounced his royal robes to become a Buddhist monk but that is another story.

Chinese sources would have us believe that the whole of this region encompassing present day Thailand, Cambodia, Vietnam and Laos was composed of small city states frequently in conflict with each other and that earlier Chinese references to the territory known as Funan changed from about the 6th century to Chenla, one part of which was ruled successively by three Kings Bhavavarman, Mahendravarman and Isanavarman and the other (western) part by the Mons of a kingdom known as Dvaravati. These sources indicate that future generations of Khmer rulers may have originated(via the the Indian connection), in Indonesia or Java, and this, through trade, gave the Khmers their primary cultural contacts introducing them first to Hinduism and later, Buddhism, from Sri Lanka. It is significant that the Indian word for millet is Yava and in ancient times Java was known as Yava Dwipa or the Island of Millet.

As far as can be gauged, Funan (1st or 2nd Century AD) was the earliest Hindu kingdom in contemporary Cambodia. Chinese accounts speak of "more than a thousand Brahmanas who reside there" and of the people of Funan who "follow their doctrines and give them their daughters in marriage. They read their sacred books day and night." The Khmers obviously had their own deities but preferred to subordinate these to the new doctrines without disputing them or proposing new ones. The Hindu domination continued until the 12th Century mainly through its two principal sects—the Shaivites or the followers of Shiva and the Vaishnavites or the followers of Vishnu.

The magnificent shrine of Angkor Wat built by Surya Varman II in the 12th century, was originally dedicated to Vishnu. The name derives from the Sanskrit word "Nagar" meaning city and "Wat" which is the Khmer word for temple. It stands on top of a tiered terraced structure. Each terrace forms a kind of covered gallery reminiscent of the Pallava architecture of South India, adorned with sculptures and bas reliefs leading to the next higher level. The third and last gallery is 180 feet high and the central shrine with a tower rising to 213 feet and four lesser ones, dominate the entire landscape. Inside are four cruciform cloisters with tanks which connect to the temple's different levels. The whole complex, facing west, is 2/3rds of a mile from east to west and ½ a mile from north to south. It is surrounded by a stone wall with ornamental gates, similar, though not identical, to the "gopurams" of South India, and a 700 foot wide moat bridged by a stone causeway with balustrades and guardians in the form of lions and multiheaded nagas. There are differences of opinion why the temple faces west. The most likely explanation is that it was dedicated to Vishnu who is sometimes associated with the West. Angkor Wat is in short, a microcosm of the Hindu concept of the Universe. The moat represents the mythical oceans and the concentric galleries, the mountain ranges surrounding the tallest of them, Mount Meru, home of the Gods.

Ta Prohm, known for the gigantic fig and silk cotton trees that engulf the temple and, over thousands of years are now intertwined with the ruins, was chosen by the Ecole Francaise d'Extreme Orient to be left in its "natural state". Located south of Angkor Wat in the direction of Angkor Thom it also features concentric galleries and towers, mainly in a dilapidated state. However the trees which have grown roots deep into the soil are its most spectacular feature. They at once protect the structures and are also agents of destruction when felled by a storm, or die. The temple was built by Jayavarman VII who converted to Buddhism. Its principal deity, Prajnapati (the Perfection of Wisdom) was created in the likeness of the King's mother.

King Jayavarman VII also founded Angkor Thom, earlier known as Nagaradham another temple city a few kilometres south of Angkor Wat. Jayavarman began his reign after defeating and driving out the Chams who had mounted a surprise naval attack on the kingdom. During his 30 year rule he undertook one of the largest building programmes ever undertaken. The central feature of the grand temple of Bayon was its forty odd towers, dominated by a central tower, nearly 150 feet high. Each tower has a finely carved human face on four sides, representing what many scholars consider to be Shiva, deep in meditation. However, considering its Buddhist antecedents there are other interpretations including one that suggests that these faces were sculpted in the king's own image. Bayon is approached after visiting several other massive secular structures surrounding it, namely the Terrace of the Elephants and the Terrace of the Leper King—reception pavilions surrounding the Royal Square of Angkor Thom where visiting dignitaries were presented to the king. The latter derives its name following an old folk legend that one of Angkor's kings was a leper. Angkor Thom was the largest of all the Khmer cities. Its magnificent South Gate with four towers and faces pointing in each of the cardinal directions, is preceded by an equally impressive avenue of Devas and Asuras churning the ocean as they sit on either side of the bridge across the moat.

About 20 kilometres north of Angkor is the beautiful temple of Banteay Srei and the temples of the Roluous Group. Banteay Srei is routinely described as the "Jewel of Khmer Art." The name, possibly derived from the Sanskrit "Sree" to denote beauty, grace and good fortune is also referred to as the "Citadel of Women" or "Citadel of Beauty". It was built out of pink sandstone and dedicated to Tribhuvana Maheswara or Shiva, the Great Lord of the Threefold World. Guide books say the central and southern sanctuaries were dedicated to Shiva while the northern was dedicated to Vishnu. However it does not require much imagination to conclude that these shrines were probably dedicated to the Hindu triad of Brahma, Vishnu and Maheshwara. The temple built by one of King Rajendravarman's counsellors and completed in 967 AD just one year before the king died, abounds in beautiful sculptures of Apsaras and sandstone relief carvings on panels and lintels. Close by is the temple of Preah Ko built in the 9th Century by IndravarmanI and dedicated to Shiva. One of its shrines was dedicated to Parameswara, the Supreme Lord, another name for Shiva and in this case, also the posthumous title of the founder of the Khmer empire, Jayavarman II.

The enormity and sublime beauty of these monuments apart, all of the temples described above, carry intricate sculptures, bas reliefs and panel carvings conveying the message of the triumph of good over evil, whether it is through mythological episodes like Vishnu's churning of the ocean or of Krishna as one of Vishnu's avatars—his killing of the demon Kansa, or tearing apart the naga Kaliya, or Krishna as Arjuna's charioteer in the Mahabharata helping the Pandavas to defeat the Kauravas. Stories from the Ramayana the other and most widely known Hindu epic are also depicted in panel after panel—the abduction of Sita, the conquest of Lanka, the fight between Bali and Sugriva, Ravana shaking Mount Kailash and many others. Not much can be learnt about the lives of ordinary people except from a series of carvings on the outer gallery walls of the Bayon. These illustrate royal victories and offerings to the king by his subjects, processions, markets, wearing apparel (the women like the men wore only a strip of cloth round the waist), household scenes and everyday occurrences.

Buddhism made its first major appearance in Cambodia in the 12th Century following the accession of Jayavarman VII, although Vajrayana Buddhism (a form of Tantric worship in which esoteric beliefs and rituals involving female divinities) seems to have been practised in some parts of the region as early as 7th Century AD.

Mahayana Buddhism with its numerous Bodhisattvas (followers of the faith who had voluntarily halted their progress to Buddhahood), came later. Buddha is now worshipped in one of the sanctuaries of Angkor Wat and Bayon features many Buddhist motifs. The Prasats Chrung—four sandstone temples at each corner of Angkor Thom are all dedicated to Bodhi sattva Lokesvara. Preah Khan, also in Angkor Thom, was more than a temple. It was a Buddhist University with over 1000 teachers. Buddhist symbolism is also in evidence Neak Pean and several other shrines in the area. After the rise of Theravada Buddhism (the current form practised in Cambodia) in the 13th century only wooden Buddhist temples seem to have been made. As most of these structures perished with time, it is not possible to accurately trace the rise of Buddhism after the 13th Century. Nevertheless the Angkor Kingdom lasted until the end of the 16th Century.

That the Khmer people have today recovered from the atrocities of the Khmer Rouge is in itself a miracle. Emotionally Angkor and its surrounding countryside is a monument to their courage and determination. The Khmers speak glibly of being forcibly taken away from their homes to serve the militants, of relatives being shot at point blank range and of a whole generation permanently mutilated by land mines. Notwithstanding extreme poverty, they gaze at visitors with a habitual expression of friendliness tinged with the wisdom of old settlers. There are no older persons in Angkor, and no secrets, or illusions for a child. By the time he is six he already has the gestures, the expressions and a fair amount of the specific knowledge of an adult. Here is a society where, thanks to the massacres, women are at a premium—it is the groom's family that pays the dowry—a society, tucked away from the humdrum of metropolitan life, glad to be alive and proud of its traditions.

*   *   *